THE Journey OF PARENTING

*Helping Your Child Become
A Competent, Caring, Contributing Adult*

LINDA S. BUDD, PHD, LP, LMFT, RPT-S

Copyright © 2011 Linda S. Budd, PhD
All rights reserved.

ISBN: 1460902645
ISBN-13: 9781460902646
Library of Congress Control Number: 2011902062

Contents

Acknowledgements vii

My Mission ix

Chapter One 1
How Do I Know if I'm on the Right Track?
- How can I tell if I'm unintentionally undermining my goals for my child's development?
- How can I ensure my child's happiness?
- What are the four developmental channels of effective parenting?
- How will I know if I'm on the right track?

Chapter Two 9
How Do I Begin and Continue the Journey to Security?
- How do I make my child feel secure?
- How does security change over time?
- How does the larger world affect security?
- What are some rituals that will help my child feel secure?
- Can security be lost and regained?
- Are there signs or channel markers that let me know I'm still in the channel?
- What interferes with my helping my child feel secure?
- Conclusion

Chapter Three 43
**How Do I Begin and Continue
the Journey to Protection?**
- Why is protection so important for my child?
- What does protection look like within my child?
- How does protection change over time?
- What interferes with helping my child feel protected?
- Are there rituals that can help my child feel protected?
- What signs or channel markers let me know I'm still in the channel?
- Can protection be lost and regained?
- Conclusion

Chapter Four 75
What Is Important about Feeling Important?
- What does importance look like within my child's and my relationship?
- How does importance change over time?
- What interferes with my child feeling an appropriate level of importance?
- Can importance be lost and regained?
- Are there rituals that can help my child feel important?
- What channel markers let me know I'm still in the channel?
- Conclusion

Chapter Five 101
How Do I Help My Child Gain Respect?
- What is respect?
- How does respect change over time?
- Can respect be lost and/or regained?
- What are some rituals that can help my child feel respected?
- Are there channel markers that let me know if I'm still in the channel?
- What interferes with my child feeling respected?
- Conclusion

Chapter Six............................**135**
**How Do I Use This Information
to Reach My Goal?**
- What questions do I need to ask?
- How does parenting style change over time?
- What does my child bring to the equation?
- Conclusion

References........................**153**

Acknowledgements

This work is like a child that has taken a village and seemingly many lifetimes to raise. I am especially grateful to my husband, Jeff Budd, whose belief in my work was my compass that kept me on my course. Scott Edelstein has been a constant, often helping me see my way through to each new step. I thank Tom Wright who offered many supportive suggestions. Tamara Kaiser, Kathy McClure and Heather Tibbles-Vassilev each served as editors before it went to press. I am grateful for their honest feedback.

Finally I must thank the many families and children who have helped me learn over the last 35 years. I have been and will always be honored by their belief in me. All of the examples in the book are based on personal and professional experiences. The characteristics of each example are combinations of many of these experiences, not related to any one family's story. Outside of these examples, I refer to children as "he" or "she" interchangeably, changing from one pronoun to the other to present my ideas in a manner that is not gender specific.

My Mission

For over thirty years—all my adult professional life—I have studied parenting, taught parenting, written about parenting, parented my own two daughters, and guided countless other children and parents in my work as a psychologist, marriage and family therapist, and play therapist. When I wrote *Living with the Active Alert Child*, I was trying to help parents with children who had previously been considered difficult. They were indeed difficult to parent. Only a few of the many ideas in other parenting books really worked with them. I found these children to be creative and delightful. I wrote to help parents recapture the feeling of delight about their child and to help families work together to bring out the best in their children.

Times have changed. Parents have changed. I see young parents going to the Internet to get ideas about how to solve a particular problem with their child and in the process doing what I call "answer grabbing." As a professional who knows many techniques to solve specific parenting problems, I began to believe something was missing. Each set of parenting techniques is derived from its own set of assumptions about the nature of the child and the child's development. For a parenting technique to really work, you must understand how it was developed—what assumptions the originator held about the nature of the child and the parent-child relationship. All techniques are based on specific beliefs about the relationship between the nature of children and parenting. Many parents try a technique without understanding whether its underlying assumptions are aligned with their own beliefs.

This relationship aspect is commonly missing from the process when a frustrated or scared parent seeks to find a quick and easy solution to a problem. Because the relationship is missing, it is easy to overlook the larger picture of what the child is learning. For logical consequences to work, there must first be encouragement from the parent. For time-out to work, the parent must have spent most of his time reinforcing the behavior he wants. It is my hope to provide a view of that relationship. My goal is for you to understand the relationship between what you are teaching your child now and what you want your child to learn in order to become a competent, caring, and contributing adult.

In the last few years, I have seen parents read about techniques, such as logical consequences, time-out, or 1-2-3 Magic. Because they did not fully understand the relationship picture, sometimes the ideas worked, and sometimes they did not. Parents often took the technique and used it simply to try to control their child. Unfortunately, they did not understand that the technique would work only in the context of a positive relationship with the child. Parents sometimes had expected the child to control himself when the parents did not really control themselves. They did not see the example they were setting. I truly believe each parent does the best he or she can; therefore, the above is not meant to criticize parents. This is simply a wake-up call.

My work is meant to be an overarching umbrella for parents. It is meant to outline the mission or goal of parenting. Within the umbrella, once that relationship is established, choices will become clearer. The choice of how to problem solve will be based upon facilitating the mission we all have as parents—helping children become competent, caring, and contributing adults.

CHAPTER ONE
How Do I Know if I'm on the Right Track?

How can I tell if I'm unintentionally undermining my goals for my child's development?

We all want our children to feel loved and to be happy. We also want them to become competent, caring, and contributing adults—adults who continue to feel loved and be happy.

We dream about this future for our children and envision them competently navigating life's good times and challenges (with, perhaps, an occasional call to us for advice). We see them as people who care about others and whom others like and care about. And we see them as people who don't just do things for themselves, but contribute to the world around them. This might mean caring for their own children, building rewarding professional careers, or being supportive friends.

Parents can actually disable their children and prevent them from growing up into competent, caring, contributing, happy adults. Many parents unwittingly undermine the attainment of these goals for their children. Parents unintentionally do things that contribute to their child becoming more dependent as opposed to more independent, becoming more self-absorbed rather than more caring, and prevent them from learning how their behaviors affect those they love, etc. How can you tell if you are unintentionally undermining your child's development? How might you be contributing to the very problems you worry about in your child?

Let me share a true story of well-intentioned parents who actually are unwittingly contributing to their child's problems and not helping their child.

Siri is a four-year-old little girl with big brown eyes. She is an only child, and the apple of both her mother's and father's eyes. Her father adores her and frequently tells her how pretty, smart, and funny she is. Her mother, who stays home with her full-time, loves Siri completely but is overwhelmed by her tantrums. Mom complains that when she drops her off at preschool Siri screams. "If you leave me here, I won't eat my snack." At home, Siri frequently has tantrums if she does not get her way. Mom, who is tired and feels like a failure, wants Siri to be happy. Siri frequently is unhappy "no matter what I do." Often Siri will tell her mother, "If you loved me, you would let me…"

Siri is a very bright child who has learned that it is important to Mom and Dad that she feel loved and be happy. Herein lies the problem. To quote Viktor Frankl, "Happiness cannot be pursued; it must ensue." In other words, Siri's parents must provide their daughter with love through their trustworthiness. They need to provide her with consistency, routine, and structure, but it is up to Siri to pursue happiness. There will be times she will feel happy and times she will not. The goal of her parents must be to provide the tools Siri needs in order to make herself happy (i.e., regular sleep, food, and a life with structure). It is Siri's job to use the tools. We will talk in the upcoming chapters about what these tools are and how parents can provide them. We will also discuss the dilemma parents face given children's different temperaments, intelligences, and disabilities. These other variables can affect how quickly your child learns to use the tools you as the parents provide.

How can I ensure my child's happiness?

The truth is that we parents can't make our children happy. If we buy them the latest and greatest things and send them off to the amusement park every day for fun galore, it won't make them happy. In fact, it will have the opposite effect. They will learn to expect the latest and greatest toy and amusement park rides every day. When they don't get them, they will feel unhappy and unloved.

Successful parents are intentional parents. They have a goal of raising their children to be competent, caring, contributing adults. Once this goal is achieved, their child's happiness, as well as their own, will naturally follow.

In order to reach this goal, of course, successful parents must navigate a lengthy voyage through the potentially treacherous waters of childhood, adolescence, and early adulthood.

One of the big challenges in this journey is that children are always growing and changing, as are family dynamics. Parents learn early that they cannot force their children to become competent, caring, and contributing. Viktor Frankl wrote, "A forced intention makes impossible what one forcibly wishes."

Since we can't make our children happy or force them to become successful adults, what *are* we parents to do?

The answer is to love our children and not let our desires for their happiness or our fears, such as a fear of conflict with them, prevent us from helping them to become competent, caring, and contributing adults.

This may sound simple, but it isn't.

No parenting book can provide its reader with answers for every situation that may arise. So, instead, I will share with you a comprehensive, easy-to-understand developmental model that will enable you to understand your child's behavior as well as his developmental needs.

By means of this model, I will introduce you to the four developmental channels through which you and your child must sail. I will point out the warning signs that indicate when you or your child is sailing off course. I will explore other factors, such as our fears, our competing interests, and our own egos that so easily interfere with us as a parent steering the boat back on course. I will also challenge you to get past your own issues in order to make the needed course corrections.

What are the four developmental channels of effective parenting?

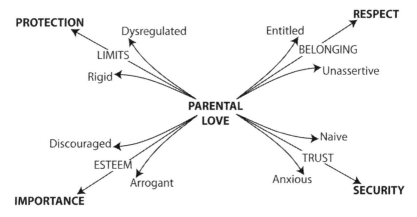

The four developmental channels, as derived from Erik Erikson, are: *security*, *protection*, *importance*, and *respect*. By successfully navigating these four channels with your child, you can be assured that she will feel loved.

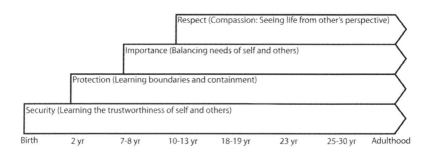

HOW DO I KNOW IF I'M ON THE RIGHT TRACK?

Security is provided by consistency. When children are treated consistently, they learn that they can trust their parents. Infants need to be able to trust their parents to know that when they are hungry, they will be fed. Infants also need to know that when they are wet, they will be changed. They need to know that when they are tired, they will be soothed to sleep. As the child becomes a toddler, competent parents restructure their daily lives to continue to meet the child's needs in a consistent and reliable way. As the child gets older, he becomes more independent, but his need for consistency continues. When parents stop to shop for groceries after picking their child up from day care, this unexpected change may create problems, especially if the child is tired and hungry. This may not seem like a big deal, but it disrupts the child's routine. If the child is tired and hungry, the change of routine may not go well. As the child grows, the ways to provide security will also change.

Protection means not only protecting the child from outside threats, such as cars in the street, but also protecting her from herself and her own willfulness. All children naturally test rules, limits, and expectations. When you hold to these firmly with calm assurance, you provide your child with emotional protection. By calmly reassuring your child that you will help her learn to regulate her own emotions, you provide her with both protection and security.

Children learn *importance* when their parents recognize and acknowledge their strengths and help them address their weaknesses. This also helps them build self-esteem. Children learn they are important when their parents make time for them, play with them, and share the tasks of daily life with them.

However, if a child needs to keep everyone's attention, he has learned that he is overly important. For this reason, parents need to teach their children that attention must be shared with others.

Finally, parents need to *respect* their children as well as teach them to respect others. When children are expected to contribute to their family and community, they feel respected and sense that they have a place of value and belonging. This is true whether the contribution involves taking their dirty dishes to the sink at four or five, setting the table at six or seven, emptying the dishwasher at nine or ten, making their own school lunch at twelve or thirteen, or volunteering at the nearby community center at fourteen or fifteen. Through such actions, the child both gains the respect of his family members and gains his own self-respect.

How will I know if I'm on the right track?

Each of the four developmental channels—*security*, *protection*, *importance*, and *respect*—have channel markers or warning buoys that serve to alert parents when they are drifting out of the channel. These markers are guidelines to help parents chart their children's course down these waterways toward healthy adult lives. Venture too far from the center of any channel, and there will be problems for both you and your child.

The channel markers in this book are indicators of potential problems. They are descriptions of your child's behavior that tell you that either you or your child is veering off course. These channel markers are not meant to assign blame to anyone; some children and indeed some parents are naturally disposed to veering off course. Such markers are simply signs that warn us of potential danger. They are the signs that the parenting boat could become grounded on a shoal. A shoal is a place that is too shallow for boats. The shoal is not a healthy or safe place to be.

The first time you see a particular channel marker in your or your child's life, take note. The second time it appears, your child may be nearing the edge of the channel. If it appears a third time, your child is in danger of getting stuck on the shoals. At this point, she needs increased, considered, and intentional parental involvement to sail back into the center of the channel.

This book is about hope—the hope that we can learn about our parenting, learn about our children, renew our goals, and intentionally raise our children with love. Love of our children allows us to honestly look at how we might be contributing to our children drifting out of the channel (i.e., moving away from becoming competent, caring, and contributing adults). We all make mistakes, but we can still be good enough parents, simply by correcting our course. Learning how to determine what it is we do that may have unintended consequences helps each of us become the best parents we can be.

It is my goal to help you with your own child, enabling you to parent from love. Parental love is courageous and self-correcting. Parents make adjustments, just as sailors constantly correct the course of their boats to account for the current, the wind, channel depth, etc.

In the following chapters, I invite you to sail with me on the great journeys of parenting and growing up. Along the way, I will point out the treacherous waters, the shoals on either side of each channel. I will share stories of people who have gotten beached in various spots along the way. If you or your child has gotten beached on the shoals, I'll help you get off those shoals and resume sailing in the right direction once again.

I am honored to be your guide to that place of love and health for both you and your child.

CHAPTER TWO
How Do I Begin and Continue the Journey to Security?

When we are granted the gift of a little person to care for and mentor into adulthood, our first task is to help her feel safe and assure her we are reliable; we are there for her. We want our children to feel secure. In that way, they learn that adults are trustworthy and eventually learn they can trust themselves.

Security is Horton the Who. Horton means what he says 100 percent in Dr. Seuss's *Horton Hatches an Egg*. Lazy Mayzie asks Horton to sit on her egg while she takes a break. What Mayzie doesn't say is that she is going to Florida for the winter. Horton sits on her egg waiting for her to return.

> And then came the winter
> …the snow and the sleet!
> And icicles hung
> From his trunk and his feet,
> But Horton kept sitting
> and said with a sneeze,
> "I'll stay on this egg
> and I won't let it freeze.
> I meant what I said
> And I said what I meant…
> An elephant's faithful
> One hundred percent!"[1]

---

1 Dr. Seuss, *Horton Hatches an Egg*.

How do I make my child feel secure?

Trust is the current that pushes the parenting boat down the channel and allows the child to build a sense of security.

An infant needs to establish a sense of trust in the world. Trust is built when care is provided to the child by parents in a consistent manner. When he is hungry, he is fed. When he is wet, he is changed. The child develops hope by receiving care and learning to give care in return throughout life. As the child grows and provides more care for himself, he still needs to feel secure in your consistent love for him. He needs to know he will continue to be loved as he learns the lessons of life, even though he may make mistakes along the way. This sense of security within the child helps him feel he is enough. In other words, he is good enough to deserve care, to deserve love.

In the case of one child, Eli, the inconsistency that followed the divorce of his parents led to insecurity.

> **Eli's Insecurity**
> Mom and Dad are divorced. With the divorce, Mom had to return to work. Their son, Eli, who is three and a half years old, attends an all-day preschool. The preschool teacher reports to Mom that Eli becomes sad and scared at the end of the day. He told her that he is not certain who will pick him up. Many things have changed since Eli's parents separated six months earlier. He used to be at home with Mom all day. Now she works; he goes to school. Some days, Mom picks him up; sometimes it's Dad; and sometimes it's Grandpa.

At three and half years of age, it is Eli's parents' job to provide consistency, taking into account his needs. They could not have predicted their marriage would dissolve. It is no one's fault. They saw several therapists and could not find happiness together. However, this has clearly disrupted Eli's sense of security—too many

HOW DO I BEGIN AND CONTINUE THE JOURNEY TO SECURITY?

changes. Both the parents and grandparents love Eli. The question is: how can Eli's family establish routines and structure in this new world in a way that honors Eli's needs for security? At such a young age, Eli cannot provide his own sense of security. They address his need for security by making pictures of his caregivers and laminating them. Each day, Mom attaches the picture of the person who will pick Eli up to his backpack. The teacher reports that Eli has a much better late afternoon these days.

The parents work well together for Eli's benefit, and the parenting boat is now moving back into the channel.

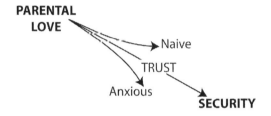

As we see in the security model above, there are two directions a child can take away from the channel of security. The shoal off the channel on one side is anxiety.

> **Mia's Anxiety**
> Mia lives with her mother and visits her Dad. Mom and Dad divorced when she was three years old. Mia constantly complains when she has to visit Dad. Dad is a loving father, but Mia has never handled change well. Mia is very attached to her mother. Mom says she felt abused by Dad in the marriage, and she worries a lot about Mia when she is with Dad. Dad is very gentle to Mia when he brings her to the office. Mia never talks about him in her play in any way that makes me believe she is unsafe with him. However, Mia frequently complains to Mom about Dad not doing something

> for her, about the day-care adult being mean, or other children who are mean to her. Mom listens and is worried about Mia while she is away from her.
> When Mia started first grade, her teacher noticed she had brought a cell phone with her to school. Mom had told Mia to call her if she was upset by the teacher or her classmates.

Mom loves Mia and is worried for her, but one of her goals should be to gain awareness of how her actions affect her daughter's sense of security. By supplying a phone to Mia, the message Mom is giving is that the school, the teacher, and her classmates are not trustworthy. The ultimate, unstated message that Mia may also receive is: "I [her Mom] am untrustworthy because I send you all day to unsafe places." These are not messages that are helpful to Mia. To be able to grow into a healthy adult, she will need to learn that most adults and classmates in this world are trustworthy. Mom's actions need to be consistent with that message. Mom could observe the school and teacher before Mia begins. She could then assure Mia how she chose this special place just for her.

Do not think this is all Mom's fault. Mia was born with a slow-to-warm-up, more anxious temperament. Mom has become very anxious, if she wasn't already, because of the divorce and constant feedback from Mia. Both need to be lovingly guided into a more secure place.

On the other side of the channel of security, a child can stray toward an overly trusting, and potentially dangerous, naïveté.

> ### Laurel Is Too Trusting
> Laurel is the second-born in a family with two daughters. Mom and Dad work around each other's schedules and are always there for their girls. Laurel is two and a half and has been taking swimming lessons with Mom or Dad since she was six months old. She

has no fear of the water. Lately, she has started to run around the pool and just assume Mom or Dad will be there when she jumps in.

Too great a feeling of security can be dangerous. In Laurel's case, this is a good time to teach some caution (mistrust)—Laurel is too secure and trusts herself and grown-ups too much. She must learn there are times and places, such as the swimming pool, where she should not feel entirely secure. As in all things, a balance is required.

Parents need to be there consistently, time after time, when an infant is hungry or needs comfort. Given that parents may not always be able to do this themselves, they must choose a loving, consistent caregiver when they can't be there. As the child grows, she gains more and more experience that can be translated into a feeling that the world is a safe, secure place. She thinks, *I can trust my parents*, and potentially later trust the world.

There is a place where we trust others too much but do not learn to trust ourselves. On the same side of the channel where naïveté lurks also lies the shoal of dependency. Bruce's story at the end of this chapter is a good example of such dependency at a later age, whereas Bethany is dependent at five years old.

Bethany's Dependence

Bethany is five years old and lives with two younger siblings and her mother and father. Both parents work.

Bethany has selective mutism. She refuses to speak to anyone other than her siblings and parents. Once in a while, she whispers to her grandmother.

Bethany is scheduled soon to be tested for entrance into kindergarten. Herein lies the problem. It is difficult to test a child's readiness for kindergarten if she will not speak. The preschool teacher refers her family to my office.

> Before I meet Bethany, I observe her at her preschool. She looks like a well-groomed five-year-old. Her teacher reports Bethany has been in her class for five months and has yet to speak to her. When Bethany needs something, she whispers to her favorite friend, who speaks for her. Her friend just says, "Oh, that's Bethany; she doesn't talk to anyone." Children are so accepting, and the class seems to have adapted to Bethany not talking.

If you are a selective mute, you have made yourself dependent on a select few other people to speak for you. This means you must place great trust in these people and little trust in yourself. To help Bethany, I must help her see that other people are also trustworthy and that she must trust herself.

When bringing Bethany to my office, her mother had said she was coming to "a talking doctor." Since children who manage to quit talking are also quite anxious as a group, I explain that Bethany does not have to talk to me; I am simply the play doctor.

Throughout the first several sessions, Bethany plays in my sand world. She runs her fingers through the sand. She buries the treasure chest. I simply make comments about the safety of my office and the feel of the sand. I also note that she has hidden her treasure. "You're in charge of your treasure, and you keep it safe." We repeat the same play over many sessions. When she believes my office and I provide consistency and security, she begins to speak to me. After that, I help her see that others, like her teacher, are safe.

Bethany is an example of a child running aground on both sides of the security channel. On one hand, she is too trusting of a select few individuals. On the other hand, she does not trust herself and she does not trust anyone else outside of her family or closest friend. She thus exhibits both anxiety and dependency.

In this case, Bethany's mom was also anxious and overwhelmed. Mom and Dad had to learn how to be more consistent and build structure and routine into Bethany's home life. Mom also learned how her own anxiety affected her ability to be consistent with Bethany.

How does security change over time?

I have stated that the mission for parents, in order to love their child, is to provide security, protection, importance, and respect for the child. These tasks change over time; there is a gradual hand-off from parent to child as the child approaches adulthood. In the beginning, you, as the parent, are the major source of security, but as children grow, they must also learn to keep themselves secure. The same is true for all the other elements, such as protection, importance, and respect. Ultimately, although we, as parents, continue to provide all the elements of love to our children throughout their lives, by adulthood, they need to be providing them for themselves.

Below is the navigational chart for the channel of security. Notice that in the beginning of the journey of security, the parent supplies the consistency that builds trust for the infant. As the child grows, she must learn over time how to supply her own consistency even through times of change and adversity. By adulthood, she must have developed the ability to trust herself to learn from life's lessons and to understand who can and cannot be trusted. This is not simply a linear process; it involves an interaction between the parent and child and ultimately between the child and the larger world. There are often two steps forward and then one to two steps backward.

On this journey, if the parent provides too much consistency and restricts access to the larger world for too long, the child may end up on the shoals of naïveté and/or dependency. On the other side of the channel, the parent must be aware of what happens if the child experiences only inconsistency and untrustworthiness. In this case, the child becomes grounded, through perpetual mistrust, on the shoals of anxiety. This is especially likely if he has a genetic predisposition to anxiety.

Security

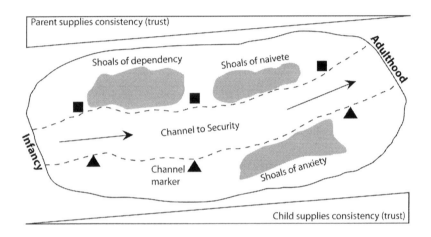

In the above diagram, I depict how the process of parenting changes over time and over the course of your child's development. I also show the shoals upon which the parenting boat will become stuck when the balance between parent and child does not change over time.

In the channel of security, overly protective (helicopter) parents need to be careful they do not create a child who is naïve about the world or too dependent. The child may not have been allowed to test his own ideas of the world and may have trusted when trust should not have been extended. He may overly trust himself and his abilities; he may believe he is nothing if he does not become the next Bill Gates. This may unintentionally strand the child in the land of hopelessness and depression or a land of resentment and anger. On the other side, a child who has not received enough security or has been mistrusted may carry a constant fear and anxiety, seeing little to trust in the world.

HOW DO I BEGIN AND CONTINUE THE JOURNEY TO SECURITY?

How does the larger world affect security?

The larger world of adults is very busy today. Often, both parents work in jobs that demand more than forty hours per week. As parents, we forget to slow down and meet a basic need of the child, a need for consistency. Recently, a mother asked me what was wrong with her five-year-old son, who had thrown a fit at the shopping center. As I asked questions about her son and his day, I learned she had picked him up at school, and then she and her husband had met at a large department store to buy a new mattress. Her son threw a fit at 7:00 PM after telling her several times he was hungry. He was not a bad child, just a hungry child who was used to eating at 6:00 PM, and he was tired. Being consistent in this case does not mean always staying home (having a boring family life). Some inconsistency is fine; however, the child must know that in all cases, his physical needs will be met. The parents might have stopped at the mall to eat with their son and made it a special time before shopping for a mattress.

Because of the sheer speed at which we are living, we sometimes forget there is a need to help our child believe in the future. To feel secure, an older child needs to believe he has a future; that the world outside of the home will provide him with the potential for a happy life. Today, adults are fearful about our world and our future; this does not communicate a sense of hope to our children. There have always been turbulent times in our planet's history. Society and media often give us and our children an unhealthy dose of discouragement. We have studies that suggest the amount of television an adult watches correlates strongly to the adult's level of paranoia. Paranoid people are not hopeful; they are fearful. If the television is turned off during the news, if adults become more active in groups that are working on solutions and good deeds, children will learn hope and empowerment.

If we cannot offer our children hope that we are enough to help the world with its problems, how can they believe they will be enough? What and how early are we exposing our children to the problems of the world? The balance has shifted in recent years, with children learning to mistrust rather than trust adults in their world.

What are some rituals that will help my child feel secure?

Rituals create consistency, which creates security. These rituals could be part of a religious faith, such as the celebration of Christmas, Hanukah, Ramadan, etc. They could occur once a year, or they could be daily, such as a blessing before eating. They also can be nonreligious, like the bedtime rituals of patting a child's back, the kisses when parting, and certain rhymes or phrases, such as, "Good night; sleep tight; see you in the morning light; don't let the bedbugs bite" and "I love you."

I still never depart from my adult daughters without giving them the kisses that represent the blessings of their grandmothers and grandfathers. They know I am asking all the grandmothers and grandfathers from the north, south, east, and west to go with them and protect them. This has been a ritual from when they were little and going to sleep up until today when they are adults and I leave to go home after a visit.

Each family needs to create its own story and its own rituals. I point out to my clients that when my daughter was little, I would say as I pointed to her forehead between her eyes. "I am always with you. Here." This began when she was little and saw the movie, *E.T.* In the movie, E.T. had to return to his planet to be healthy. He left Elliot with this touch. Many other parents have adopted this or a similar ritual.

Children's literature is full of examples of rituals to say to a small person, "I am with you." One such example is in *I Love You Forever* by Robert Munsch. The mother follows a son over his life cycle in pictures and is always saying, "I'll love you forever...I'll like you for always...As long as I'm living, my baby you'll be."

Rituals can also be as simple as doing the same thing with a child every day. My husband would get up with our daughters each school day at the same time and go through the same process of making breakfast and lunch while simultaneously listening to a National Public Radio news show. Our youngest would come down to the kitchen to eat after dressing every day and be greeted with, "Hello, I'm Carl Castle." Over twenty years later, she still fondly remembers this ritual.

What are your particular family rituals? They may involve words or just acts that mean "We are a family, and I will be there for you."

For many children in divorced families, I encourage the parents to create a tradition on the first night the child transitions back to a new household. For example, if she goes to a new household on Sunday night, they can create a tradition of snacks and a program they all watch as a family to help the children reenter their other family.

Can security be lost and regained?

Security is worked on throughout life. It is the development of trust—trust of other and trust of self. Trust of other is first gained by consistent caregiving in infancy. However, as the child leaves the parent and goes to day care, to preschool, and to school; changes school; or goes to college, trust is up for renegotiation. As the world expands, the question of our trustworthiness must be reconsidered. Each trusting experience builds a reservoir within the child. Therefore, each "trusting of other" experience, whoever the other may be, adds to that reservoir within the growing person. Needless to say, the reservoir is diminished by encounters with adults who are not trustworthy.

The same can be said about trust in self. As a child walks off to preschool, does she feel like she can be successful? Can she trust herself to do the things that are asked of her? I have seen children scarred deeply by one or two different teachers in elementary school who did not understand them, who did not encourage them. What the teacher did not understand may have been a learning style or a learning disability. The children came away fearing they could not trust themselves to do schoolwork well.

The stakes become higher as the child grows. The transition into junior high or middle school may be somewhat scary; his transition into high school even scarier. The transition to college, not only the level of work but leaving his family, is a terrifying time of renegotiating trust of self. Can he really do this? Finally, can he trust himself enough to choose a partner for a lifetime?

```
Security (Learning the trustworthiness of self and others)
     ○        ○        ○        ○        ○        ○
Birth   2 yr    7-8 yr   10-13 yr  18-19 yr  23 yr   25-30 yr  Adulthood
```

The chart above represents security over the child's life cycle. The circular flow symbols indicate normal times a child might revisit whether he or his parent is trustworthy. However, please keep in mind life events that are not predictable would also yield circles not on the chart. These events might include the death of a parent, a divorce, a parent deployed to war, the illness of a sibling, a move, and many other life interruptions.

Are there signs or channel markers that let me know I'm still in the channel?

The Atlantic Intercoastal Waterway flows down the U.S. coastline from Maine to the Florida Keys and over to the Texas seaboard. To sailors, it is marked just like a highway. As you go south, red, triangle-shaped markers should stay on your right and green, square-shaped markers on your left. The markers might indicate where it is not safe when the tide is out, because the water may be too shallow. They may signal an area where the sandbar shifts or there is a rock jetty. It is not always unsafe, but you won't know whether it is passable. It is not reliable. These markers or buoys signal the safest way to proceed: "It is deep enough in this channel to support your craft." Other markers signal, "Do not go past here."

In the same way that buoys mark the safety of the waterway, there are markers that indicate a safer passage in trying to teach your child. The markers serve as guideposts to help parent-child relationships keep in safe waters. If we follow the markers that indicate safer water, our relationships grow and our children grow because they rest in deeper water. These waters can sustain this vessel that is growth.

This section is meant:
1) to offer you consistent markers so that you may notice when you have gone out of the channel, and
2) to give you simple phrases that catch your child's attention so he can navigate himself back into the channel.

I do not mean to say that these markers show the only safe passage, rather that other ways may or may not be safe. It depends upon the tides, the time of day, or the shifting sands. These markers are meant to suggest a safe, reliable passage. There are many more markers; the ones below are the ones I use most often in helping parents.

As you travel down this relationship waterway, there will be markers to help build security with your child, help build protection, help build importance, and finally help build respect. Inevitably, on a long journey, there will be storms or inclement times that the relationship will have to weather. Keep to the channel, batten down the hatches when it rains, and enjoy the warmth when it is sunny.

All the channel markers in this section are meant to build trust within your child. That trustworthiness is built by your consistency, your reliability. When parents are consistent, children learn trust in the world. As consistency is modeled for them and they are asked to be consistent themselves, they learn to trust themselves. As they are given consistency, they become less anxious about what is next. As they grow older, life's various demands dictate that schedules vary sometimes, which will help them slowly learn adaptability.

- ***Security Channel Marker #1: If you're bored as parents, you're probably doing a good job.***

When my youngest daughter was in seventh grade, my husband asked me, "Just how long do we have to keep up this schedule, being here to help with homework and getting the kids to bed on time?" Remember, he was getting up with her every school morning. Then, on at least two school nights a week, I was speaking someplace, teaching, or maybe counseling. I left after he returned at 5:00 and we had eaten our family dinner. He was in charge those evenings. At that point, we'd been in the business of daily consistency for sixteen years with our oldest and helping with homework for eleven years, and he was bored. My reply was simple, "Until our daughters have the purpose of the routines internalized." Our oldest already understood what staying up late did to her body. If she had a late jazz dance class, she would say, "It's really hard to turn off my body and get to sleep on those nights." Our youngest wasn't quite there yet.

Keeping consistent routines is boring compared to the choices in life we have at our disposal. But it's that consistency that allows a child to trust and be secure in the fact that her parents honor the needs of her mind and body. It recognizes that asking a child to be adaptable all day at school and adaptable all night to her parents' whims will not work, especially for those children who are less adaptable by their very temperament.

Having routines at home diminishes power struggles over who gets to have his whims honored. It allows children downtime from the stress of everyday decisions. Some things are just done because that's what we do in our family.

I am not saying that there is no free time but that even free time can be defined by routines. For example, playdates are on Tuesdays and Thursdays after school, on Saturday afternoons, or after homework; that's when our children can choose what they do.

Getting Back in the Channel:

When you find yourself in arguments with your child about bedtime, homework, etc., it is a good indicator you are out of the channel. Your child no longer trusts you to choose her course. She probably thinks you make her do things because it is about your need for power and control, not because certain routines teach self-control. Routine and structure is boring, but until the control becomes more internalized, it beats fighting. The child will trust you to order her life if it does not seem whimsical, if it does not seem to be about meeting your inconsistent wishes. Order also makes a child less anxious since she knows what is coming next in her life. A child often fights because she is scared or anxious; she is uncertain what is next and therefore tries to take charge. She tries to control the world around her when she cannot control the anxiety within herself.

- ***Security Channel Marker #2: You get four mistakes a day.***

This chapter is about consistency and trust, which leads to the child feeling secure. One of the most important lessons on consistency you can give your child is that you trust him and that you will always love him no matter what imperfections he shows. For some parents, this lesson is hard to teach when their child has made a mistake. I say this is the perfect teachable moment.

Everybody makes mistakes. Nobody is perfect. However, we more often get to see the mistakes of the people we love and with whom we live. My rule for both children and grown-ups is you get four mistakes a day. Until you have used these up, you do not have to feel bad. Granted, on the days you make four, you feel as if you are having a pretty bad day, and on the days you make none, you are on top of the world. However, it is not whether or not we make mistakes or the number that is important. What is important is what we do with them.

First, do we own the mistake? Do we take responsibility for our mistakes? If it is simply a mistake and one of many we will make in a lifetime, it is simpler to say, "Gee, I made a mistake." What I mean is that we do not have to feel little and worthless—we just made a mistake. We all do, every day of our lives. Some mistakes are bigger than others, like the sixteen-year-old who wrecked the family car or the six-year-old who broke her mother's favorite Christmas ornament. But they are still just mistakes. Good children, good teenagers, good adults make mistakes every day.

Second, do we make amends for our mistake? The first step in making amends might be to say, "I am sorry." It may be cleaning up the mess we made. Cleaning up may actually be cleaning up the pieces of a broken item, or it may involve either working to repair the problem or paying for its repair. If it is a broken window, the child may go with you to buy the window and pay for some or all of its repair from his allowance or piggy bank. If it is a car accident, the teenager may pay for the repair or the deductible from the car insurance. He may need to meet with you or with your agent to determine if your insurance rates will go up. He may need to pay for or contribute to the rate increase, which is an additional burden for the family. As you can see, some mistakes are bigger than others. However, they are still simply mistakes. Mistakes do not always come in physical form. Some mistakes involve mistreating family members. Haven't we all had bad days and been grumpy or irritable?

The school-age child, when returning from a sleepover, may be lacking sleep and mistreat everyone. It is important to help children learn they are not bad, but they have made a mistake. It is a mistake to believe you can stay up most of the night and not be terrible to your family the next day. The parent needs to help the child understand she needs to be responsible for her own choice—staying up. The child needs to figure out what she could do with her tiredness, other than beat up family members, physically or emotionally. She needs to make a choice about tiredness; it could be going to bed, reading alone, spending time alone, or whatever replenishes her. Afterward, she needs to make amends to the family by baking some cookies, reading a joke to family members, setting the dinner table, or any of a thousand other ways to say, "I love you, and I'm sorry."

Using the four-mistake rule allows parents to relax, to allow mistakes without having to fear imminent life failure or a future life of crime for their children. Parents' consistent belief in a child's basic goodness and future of being a kind and responsible human helps a child move toward that future. Children can fulfill this parental prophecy; focusing on a positive future points a child in a right direction. When a parent becomes fearful about a child's competence, the child also becomes fearful. When a mistake is considered a bad choice, a parent can emphasize that the choice is not part of who the child is but simply a part of the learning journey on which the child is traveling.

The four-mistake rule must be held with an "Oh well" attitude. A problem occurs when the focus of one person becomes another's mistakes. The parent tires and then develops what I refer to as an "Oh my God" attitude. If you are looking for mistakes, clearly that is all you will see. It becomes a self-fulfilling prophecy that this child makes too many mistakes. To your child, this attitude means you don't trust her, and this damages her self-trust.

Balancing the "Oh well" attitude with the need to recognize when someone makes mistakes with abandon is an art form. When mistakes keep being repeated, there is a pattern that needs attention. Clearly, someone is not learning from his mistakes. In my office, if you are late to an appointment once a year, it is simply not a problem. When you are late for every appointment, it is a therapeutic issue. When a person repeatedly drives drunk, that is not a mistake but a dysfunctional choice for which the person is refusing to take responsibility. The denial is indicative of the illness of alcoholism. However, having the illness does not give you the right to make such a mistake.

Keeping a scorecard of mistakes that are inconsistent and have no pattern serves no purpose. Anytime a list of mistakes is kept in one person's brain, it implies there is a winner and a loser. It implies that one person is good and one is bad. This is not the basis of a healthy relationship whether it be parent-child, husband-wife, or adult-adult.

Joel's Mistake

Twelve-year-old Joel was on a wonderful vacation with his family in Montana. On the third day, they all stopped by the village general store. Joel had never seen a breath spray before. He didn't want to spend his money on it, so he quietly put it in his pocket. Lots of kids at school had talked about how they shoplifted. As they drove back to their rented condominium, Mom saw Joel unwrapping it in the backseat. She asked Dad to stop the car and confronted Joel. Joel admitted he had taken the breath spray. Dad turned the car around and drove back to the village store. The rest of the family waited while Joel and Mom went back into the store.

HOW DO I BEGIN AND CONTINUE THE JOURNEY TO SECURITY?

> Mom found the manager and asked him to explain to Joel how shoplifting affects the store. Joel apologized to the manager and paid for the breath spray. The time it took prevented the family from skiing that afternoon. Joel felt horrible.

The lesson Joel learned will stay with him forever. There was no need for the family to dwell on it or discuss it further, and they didn't. It was a mistake made, lesson learned, case closed.

Getting Back in the Channel:

We all have to be able to make mistakes. We are human. If those mistakes repeat time and time again, you might ask yourself what is behind such choices. If your child repeatedly makes the same mistakes, the questions to be resolved are:
1) How can I teach this better?
2) Is there something in the way of my child's learning?
3) Is there a fear on the part of the child that needs to be addressed?
4) Is my child focused on something (e.g., keeping my attention) that is interfering with his learning the lesson I want him to learn?

Concentrating on mistakes is bad for both the parent and the child. It makes the one who made the mistake feel incompetent and insecure about his belonging to the family. This insecurity may yield more mistakes in the future. The forgiveness of four mistakes a day should not, however, blind us to consistent dysfunctional patterns. Remember the need to own our mistake and make amends in some way to any person we've hurt and then learn from it.

Security is established when the child can trust us to respond consistently to his mistakes. We can forgive him, and he needs to forgive himself and do what is needed to mend relationships.

- **Security Channel Marker #3: You can't become taller by making others smaller.**
  It's not cool to be cruel.
  There is no security without trust. Hearing directly or indirectly that a person says bad things about you destroys trust. It is doubly worrisome when the person demeaning you or putting you down is one of your parents. One of the more dysfunctional practices I've seen is parents discussing the shortcomings of their child in from of him as if he wasn't present. How can he trust you are not

talking ill of him to everyone when he's not there? Perhaps this is the reason some people develop the feeling that the only way to feel good about themselves is to belittle or put down the people around them. Internally, a parent may believe "Only one of us can be good, and I am not taking the chance that you are the only good one." This is an early way children learn to mistrust their parent.

Later in school, children see this dynamic with their peers. In conversations with others, their peers subtly or directly belittle someone else, leaving them to wonder, *Do they say such things about me when they are with others?* Somehow, some children believe internally that they can feel better about themselves and make you believe you are really special because they are sharing a special insight or piece of information with you. This kind of discussion can occur in families but is especially prevalent among students in junior high and high school. It seems the only way to be in the "in group" in some schools. Whether in a family or in a school, the only way you know you are "in" is if someone else is "out." This dynamic leads to issues of security in deciding who is really trustworthy and who is not.

I would like to make a distinction between talking to a third party to gain insights into the dynamic between you and another person (e.g., a therapist or a really good friend who is good at not taking sides) and talking to a third party with the intention of belittling another or elevating yourself to that third party. The first process is useful to gain clarity and insight, so you might address a real issue directly to the party involved. The second only has hurtful, venting intentions. If you have to vent, only vent to someone who has little or no connection with your relationship.

One example of this dynamic occurred many years ago when three eighth-grade girls were riding in my car. It was a day off from school, and the excitement over the plans for the day was buzzing around the vehicle. In the middle, one girl turned to the other and said, "Did you notice how much makeup Mary was wearing yesterday at school?"

Another chimed in, "Yeah, she looked like a slut."

The third girl interrupted and said, "Let's talk about our day. People are always putting everybody down at school. We don't have to do that here."

Clearly, the last girl was right. The eighth-grade class was suffering. The situation had become so bad that many of their classmates were talking about leaving the school and going elsewhere for ninth grade.

What underlies this dynamic may be jealousy, envy, or fear that you have to prove someone else is bad so you don't end up on the bottom of the heap. Somehow, making fun of that other person or talking about her flaws is used to make you feel less flawed. However, the truth is that we are all flawed. We all make mistakes. Talking about a loved one's flaws with the intention of putting her down or using her flaws as a joke is a violation of the boundaries of the love relationship. It violates your own integrity within that relationship. It makes you untrustworthy. If you do talk about your relationship by talking about your child, the intention must be to improve that relationship by having a trusted individual serve as a sounding board for your concerns. This works both ways; neither the parents nor the children can make themselves look better by denigrating the other.

> **Trina Is Grounded**
> Sixteen-year-old Trina is mad at her parents. She lied to them about where she was going, and now they have grounded her for two weeks. She has told all of her friends that her parents are ogres and are from the "dark ages" because they try to control her life. Now that she is grounded, she can have friends in her home, but she is not allowed to go out. Her problem is nobody wants to visit her because she has told all of her friends that her parents are ogres.

Trina discovered firsthand the repercussions of speaking ill of her parents. Whether she learns to change her behavior or her attitude depends on whether her parents maintain their consistent love for her, consistent insistence on honesty, and consistent attempts to talk to Trina about her choices.

Getting Back in the Channel:

Although it is normal for teenagers to complain about their parents, they must start learning early on to view both the strengths and weaknesses of others. In families, do we emphasize everyone's weaknesses or their strengths? Is it possible for more than one child to be good? Does one parent always have to be right? Children learn inclusion and acceptance in their homes. If we had to be perfect, no one would be accepted. Ask yourself if you are putting your loved ones down. How does that make you feel? It can't make you feel good about them. If you love them, can you find ways to increase that love, not decrease it?

Putting others down in front of your child will decrease your child's sense of security. They will wonder, *If you put others down, will you put me down when I am not here?* Is it really okay to make mistakes or do you just use them to make me look bad?

What interferes with my helping my child feel secure?

There are many things that interfere with the process of helping a child feel secure. Let us explore some of them in the hopes you might identify what could be happening in your home.

- *Parents are too busy and overworked.*

As adults in today's society, we are very busy. Sometimes we are too busy and moving too fast for our child. Children are taking in the world and are learning new skills. This takes time. When we expect too much of them too quickly, they become overwhelmed.

When we move too quickly to stop and teach them, they believe they are the cause of the parents' stress. Rather it is our expectations or inconsistent expectations between parents that are the problem.

It is important to teach our children consistently how to become competent, caring, and contributing members of our society. The way to that goal is to take the opportunity when there is a teachable moment. The two parents need to be as consistent as possible in their approach to parenting. In that way, our children learn we, as the parenting team, are Horton the Who: we say what we mean, and we mean what we say.

I have the good fortune of helping many loving parents. Mari's mom mentioned to me that her husband is older than she is, and he believes children are offered too many choices. She says she parents differently than her husband. If Mari is yelling from the backseat, her husband pulls the car over and lets Mari know screaming and kicking his seat is unsafe and he will not continue driving until she can help keep the family safe. He believes Mom gives Mari too much choice when she counts to three to give Mari a chance to control herself. In this case, neither parent is wrong. It is not the counting that is the problem. The problem is whether both parents consistently follow-through with Mari, not whether there is a slight difference between them. Mari is smart enough to know the differences between her parents and to know who follows through and who does not. This is a typical impediment to providing consistent parenting. It takes time to talk about and agree on a parenting strategy. Sometimes parents feel they are too busy and overworked to reach such an agreement. Consistent follow-through provides security.

- *Parents are not aware of a child's needs at different stages of development.*

Most people do not spend a lifetime learning how children grow, learn, and develop. Many parents today do not understand that children are not simply miniature adults. A three-year-old brain is not only smaller than an adult's brain; it works differently. It is missing essential connections that allow an adult brain to function with expected maturity. Children need more sleep in infancy and preschool and then again in adolescence. Brain development can lead to predictable mental patterns in children. For example, three years old is the normal time for night terrors. Parents need to take such development time lines into account when dealing with a child's behavior. When a three-year-old needs to pick up his toys, helping him is quite normal; whereas a nine-year-old can do it all by himself if he has been taught the routine. A thirteen-year-old, because of all his internal growth and the ensuing chaos, may need to have the cleaning process explained again.

I give you the above examples so you, as a parent, can begin to examine your own assumptions. Too often, parents think that once their child learns something it never needs to be taught again. This is not a useful assumption. Learning happens throughout a lifetime, especially in the early years of life. Some lessons are learned in a linear fashion with children mostly taking steps forward but with an occasional step backward. Some learning occurs not once but many times while growing up. It is these lessons that require consistent, ongoing teaching or role-modeling to get children through the times when they have it, seem to lose it, and then need to learn it again. This is where consistency is the key.

If you are struggling with security with your child, think about what you are expecting from her. Does that expectation fit with her age? Does it fit with your child's temperament, learning style, and history? I am not saying your child should not consistently be taught life lessons. It's just that we cannot expect our child to learn and retain all lessons consistently.

I was once approached by a twenty-year-old mother asking how to teach her child not to touch her cigarettes on the coffee table. Her toddler was seventeen months old. She was slapping his hand whenever he touched the cigarettes. I suggested she put the cigarettes higher (i.e., on the counter or bookshelf). The issue for a seventeen-month-old is security, not limits. Later, as the child is testing his boundaries, she can teach limits. First, we teach security, second, the limits of our world. (Limits will be covered in the next chapter on protection.)

- *Parents have competing fears.*

Fear permeates our culture. Parents fear for both their own and their children's safety. They fear that there will be no future other than war and desolation. They fear our planet will become unfit for human habitation. They fear that they will not make enough money for retirement or for their children's college educations. Some of our fears are based at least partly in reality; others are not. Yet, even with reality-based fears, we parents must regularly demonstrate to our children the courage to walk through our fears and into the future.

Fearful parents can harm their children by undermining their sense of security. How can they feel safe if their parents feel unsafe? How can they face the future with courage? How can they learn to trust adults if they regularly receive the message that adults are unsafe or stupid? Think of how parents are depicted in pop culture.

Some children respond to their parents' fears by developing a bravado and a belief that they can handle anything. Other children sink deeply into a pit of fear, with no sense that adults can be trusted to help them out. With the best of intentions of love and protection, many parents raise their children fearfully, not realizing how this leads to undesired outcomes. In most cases, parents are driven by the same desire: to have their children succeed in life and be happy—and by the same fears: that they will not do the right things to achieve this goal. They are afraid their children will grow up as failures, and they will be failures, too. Parents fear that some people might hurt their children. Sometimes they even fear that others, be they the other parent, grandparents, or teachers, are not capable of taking care of their children to the standard they desire. This and other parental fears harm both parents and children.

One example of a fear affecting the child is when parents put tremendous pressure on their children to get good grades because the parents are scared their children won't get into a "good" college. Of course, these parents want their children to enjoy a successful future. But some of them also fear that if their children don't go to a "good" college, it may mean they are bad parents. In response, their children may think that they are not smart enough, and their parents won't love them if their grades are bad.

One way to tell if a fear is useful or not is to see if it is more about you than your child. For example, some parents fear that if their children become bored, it means they are not doing a good job as parents. Others fear that if they make a parenting mistake, it means they are failures as parents (or human beings). Still others fear their children will not fit in socially, which may lead to the parents feeling they don't fit in.

It is key for parents to understand that their fears can prevent their child from trusting himself. In recent years, parents have asked me if I think they ought to call their son's college professor to help the professor understand their son's needs. This reflects their fear that their son will fail or be denied the "good life" and that it will be because they, as parents, failed to do all they could.

Bruce Underfunctions

Bruce is a sophomore in college. He is very smart but had difficulty handing in his work on time in high school. Bruce works hard and does well but then has a pattern of just stopping. His high school teachers accommodated him by accepting late assignments even into summer months. His mother

> has been a big advocate, talking to his teachers (pressuring his teachers) to accommodate her son in this manner.
>
> Late in spring semester during his sophomore year at college, Bruce became overwhelmed with taking his exams. He did not have time to complete his study guides the way he thought he should, so he just quit and did not take two exams. He did not call his teachers or contact the learning specialist at college. He became very depressed. Mom again got on the telephone and talked to his college professors, asking them to allow him to take his exams. The semester had been done for weeks, but they listened to her and gave him another chance.

Bruce's mother is but one example of how some parents are advocating for their young adult children. My question is: When do you stop? Do you call his boss when he is twenty-three years old and explain that he became overwhelmed and that is why the project is not complete? My theory of parenting involves moving from a more hands-on parenting to a coaching style in adolescence where children do the work but you call the plays. Parents need to become mentors to their adult child, offering advice they may or may not accept.

In the case of Bruce, Mom is afraid that without a college degree, Bruce will be unhappy. He comes home depressed but does not connect his choices with his depression. Bruce is unhappy, and Mom believes it is her job to fix it. However, there are many other reasons parents are overfunctioning. Some parents believe the world is unfair and their child is still too young to handle the unfairness. Others simply fall into the trap of feeling sorry for their child. Still others are afraid their child will not attain the "good life" without their intervention. Others are afraid of other people's judgments: am I a bad mother if my child doesn't graduate from college? Some parents are afraid of being seen as wimps, "screwing up" their child's life, or just plain being a bad mom or dad. Many parents overfunction because they simply don't want to take the time or effort to teach their children the skills needed to solve their own problems.

The increasing number of fearful, anxious parents has led to a phenomenon now referred to at many universities as the "hovering" or the "helicopter" parent. Helicopter parents run interference for their child or pave their way. There are harmful consequences that result from trying to maintain a consistent, secure life for their child into adulthood rather than letting the child gradually provide his own internal sense of security. Their actions communicate a lack of trust in their child's own initiative and resourcefulness to handle his own problems. By trying to solve all his problems and showing a lack of respect for him, they do not allow him to learn how to cope with anxiety and feel the exhilaration of his own successes and the disappointment of his own failures. Instead, these anxious parents intervene, run interference, and do not allow the child to cope with his own anxiety. As a result of this overprotection, the child may get the message that he is incapable of going it alone without parental help. This is a disabling message to the child. The intention of these parents is to be helpful, but in acting from their fear, they are not helping their child into adulthood.

This overinvolvement has led some schools, like the University of Vermont, to use older students as "parent bouncers" to keep parents out of certain orientation sessions meant for students. To help parents let go, some campuses are putting on seminars for parents, such as "A Time of Holding On and a Time of Letting Go" at Northeastern University. This is intended for parents who are having trouble letting go and does not imply that the student is incapable of letting go.

In the past, colleges and universities ran on a policy of "in loco parentis." This meant it was the young adult's responsibility to handle her own problems, whether the problem was with academics or with roommates, using the university as a helper. The university was there to serve the role of a parent. It was the child's responsibility to communicate with her parent in absentia, the college or university. The policy allowed the university to work as a substitute parent in the child's transition from the nuclear family into the world at large. Now without such a policy, with fear rising, and with the skyrocketing cost of education, parents call the presidents of the university to discuss their daughter's issues, not unlike they would call an elementary school principal. That was unheard of ten years ago. Hara Estroff Marano in a 2004 *Psychology Today* article entitled, "A Nation of Wimps," asserts that parents are going to "ludicrous lengths" to prevent their children from dealing with any adversity. Learning to deal with adversity is an important part of growing into adulthood. The February 2008 issue of *Mother Jones* reported that the previous March, a West Virginia high school sophomore sued her teacher who had failed her for a late paper. The student sought damages for "loss of enjoyment of life."

Dealing with adversity, learning creative problem solving, and learning that there are things we can and cannot control are all skills that are necessary for a healthy, productive adult life. However, if we are so busy removing all adversity from our children's lives out of our fear they will fail, we only get better at the skills our children need, while they get weaker.

Remember, doing things for your children does not allow them either the opportunity to learn or the self-satisfaction of accomplishment. Although you may become better and better at these tasks, your children will not learn until they are allowed to try, make mistakes, and try again. This process allows your children to learn to trust themselves.

Many parents are afraid they are doing something wrong. They are terrified that they will cause pain to their children in a similar manner as their parents caused pain to them. They are afraid to set limits with their child, wanting to be their child's friends. Because they want to understand their child's feelings, they often get lost in feeling sorry for their child. They are afraid that somehow they may be hurting their child. They are afraid they will do something wrong, which is inevitable given the length and complexity of the parenting process.

Many of today's parents confuse their identities with those of their children. Their personal satisfaction, fulfillment, and sense of accomplishment depend on the success or failure of their children, not on their own achievement.

We are judged now on whether we have relationships with our adult children—whether we are generous and help our children as adults, be it by babysitting or by setting up educational funds for our grandchildren. We are judged by how we teach our children to relate to their elders, including their grandparents. Can we hold our head high during this journey? Can we, on most days, trust our own internal voice concerning what will lead to a competent, caring, and contributing adult?

Hanging on to our mission of helping our children become competent, caring, and contributing adults becomes particularly difficult when we see other parents making decisions that we do not believe lead to that goal. We see projects in the science fair that are obviously done by a parent. Young children have their own credit cards and cell phones. Teenagers are out partying from after school until 10:00 or 11:00 PM. Some are not even expected to be home for dinner. Children and teens portrayed on TV or in the movies are applauded and idolized for talking disrespectfully to adults and working around their "stuffy" requests.

Remember you will be held responsible if your child breaks the rules (e.g., is truant or past curfew). Given that you are the adult, the responsible party, it is best to surround yourself with others who share your mission. You will need support. Parenting is a long process with many ups and downs. Join a parenting chat group online. Go to early childhood classes. Find support in your neighborhood.

Children will make mistakes. We all do. It is no one's fault. However, if we do not learn from our mistakes, we miss an important opportunity. I often tell children, in my office, that even when they have made a very big mistake, this is normal. Mistakes are simply cues there's something for us to learn. All we need to do is own up to our mistake, make amends (i.e., say you're sorry or do something nice) to anyone we've hurt, and make a plan to not repeat the mistake.

Parents also make mistakes every day. We simply need to learn from them. Remember, children grow into the kind of adults they become both by what they are biologically given and by what they learn from us. We can take any biology-based difficulties and let that alone define our child, or we can let the child define himself by how he rises to the challenge of that difficulty. We are all deficient in some way; it's what we do with our whole self that makes or breaks our future.

Conclusion

How do I help my child feel secure? Security is built and rebuilt; we are always adding to the foundation already established. Are we, as parents, trustworthy? Are we there when we say we will be? No parent is perfect, but we must intentionally strive for consistency.

When we find our children questioning whether we mean what we say, can we make a new commitment about security and follow through with that commitment? As parents, we need to choose early in our child's life other people who also are trustworthy.

HOW DO I BEGIN AND CONTINUE THE JOURNEY TO SECURITY?

Whether these people are babysitters, teachers, or relatives, surround the child with a community of trustworthy others. Long ago, that community may have been aunts, uncles, cousins, and grandparents. Today, we often find ourselves isolated. As I point out to children, most people are really good people and would help a child in need. There are only a few who would not. In that way, I attempt to build a world with less emphasis on fears and more emphasis on the helpfulness of other people.

When your child has an encounter with someone who is not trustworthy, your presence can help her grow. The child needs to learn what it means to be a good friend as opposed to a bully and what it means to be a reliable adult as opposed to one who is unreliable. In this way, she also learns how to be a good, reliable friend and a good, reliable adult. She learns how to be trustworthy.

CHAPTER THREE
How Do I Begin and Continue the Journey to Protection?

Why is protection so important for my child?

In the parenting boat, protection is first formed through limits or boundaries: defining what is acceptable and what is not. When limits are rigid and do not take into account your child's unique temperament, needs, and developmental level, your child may become rigid. The child will become harder and harder on himself as he tries to meet what he believes are impossible expectations. However, when limits and the mood of the parent vary a lot, a child may become dysregulated. She may see little point in self-control when the parent provides little rhyme or reason or follow-through. She may not know how to demonstrate self-discipline or self-control because she has not seen them modeled by her parents. Keep in mind that the starting point of emotional self-control varies from child to child; temperament, possible illness, and other factors may mean the child begins further out of the channel than others her age.

Growth occurs when there is a balance of privilege and responsibility. Self-discipline grows in a land where self-discipline is practiced. All children, despite their temperament, etc., need to develop self-discipline to have success in relationships and in the world of work.

What does protection look like within my child?

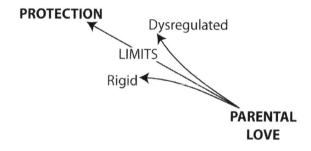

Limits propel the boat through the channel of protection. These limits include those set for the child but also those the parents set for themselves.

Within the channel of protection, a child who is rigidly contained for too long by parental limits may become a rigid adult. She will not believe in her own ability to judge right or wrong, to solve the moral dilemmas we all face in life. On the other side, a child who for too long has not experienced limits or experienced them erratically may become an adult who is emotionally and behaviorally dysregulated or out of control. We've all met adults who rage and who believe they are not accountable to either the social-respect rules of life or, worse yet, our society's law.

> **Marcus's Dysregulation**
> Mom and Dad have worked hard to provide their son Marcus with all he needs. Marcus has always been a busy boy. He's always been active and physical. Marcus was kicked out of his preschool at four. Mom and Dad have always made sure Marcus had the best helpers. When he was diagnosed with dyslexia, he got the best tutors. Marcus has been a challenge since his birth, and Mom and Dad have had difficulty giving him structure and routine.

> He has ruled the house as they tried to keep the peace. Sometimes they are better with routine, sometimes worse. Marcus was allowed to sleep wherever he fell asleep. One of the ways the parents keep Marcus scheduled is to keep him in his sport. He does both indoor and outdoor soccer.
>
> At age twelve, Marcus was between soccer programs in August. He started "hanging out" and skateboarding at the local park, coming and going as he pleased, often eating only junk food, having sleepovers at least four to five nights a week and hanging out with older boys. He believed he was in charge of himself. Marcus believed he could hang out outside until all hours despite a 10:00 PM curfew in the city. He did not feel compelled to do anything his parents wanted. Often, Marcus would call his parents names if they did not immediately agree to his requests. He was clearly bullying them. When Mom and Dad tried to set limits, Marcus escalated, and Mom or Dad became physical with him trying to contain him. Now Mom and Dad feel terrible. Marcus is outraged and feels unsafe with them.

Marcus's parents have provided him neither security nor protection. Because Marcus had such a strong will, they conceded control to him. This means he set the rules. Because his parents did not provide a calm, consistent structure that was dependable, he has come to be in charge of himself with all the pitfalls of being twelve years old. Mom and Dad need to be willing to regain their authority with Marcus without being physical. They need to demonstrate their authority through love. Love in this case would be agreement on the rules of the household and the consequences if Marcus does not follow them. The consequences are stated to let Marcus know the parents mean business. The parents will protect Marcus not only from the world but also his own will.

Once Mom and Dad make and hold to the rules with love, not anger or fear, it allows Marcus to return their love. Dad does not use physical power but reminds Marcus he is part of their family. He needs to cooperate with them in order for them to cooperate with him. Marcus has always gotten whatever he wanted (i.e., money, phones, etc.). He is helped to understand that he will have to earn those privileges by showing he can be responsible with regard to the family rules. Then the hard part comes. The parents also have to abide by those limits. If Marcus feels Mom and Dad's love for him, in their ability to set aside their anger in order to protect him, he will be more likely to set aside his own feelings for them and control his own emotions.

In the following example, Lisa represents the rigid side of the channel.

> **Lisa's Rigidity**
> Lisa is nine years old and the little sister. She is growing up with a very loving mom and dad. Her mother is a minister, and her father is a principal. Lisa's sister, who is five years older, is a great student, a superb athlete, and seems to do everything well. Lisa is active and energetic; whereas the rest of her family are all quiet readers at home. Lisa is both physically and emotionally more active, louder, etc., than her family. Lisa works to do everything right at school but often seems to be in trouble at home.

HOW DO I BEGIN AND CONTINUE THE JOURNEY TO PROTECTION?

> Lisa is a busy person in my office but a child with good boundaries and a great heart. While playing ball with me, her ball accidentally knocks over a cup of water. She immediately looks frightened and says, "I'm sorry." I assure her it is only an accident, and we proceed to wipe it up. Lisa's energy seems to have little outlet at home. If she balks at cooperating with her parents, she is seen as bad or wrong. If she makes a mistake, it is seen as a serious problem.
>
> Along with her active energy, she also has a temper. Lisa is very ashamed of her anger.

Mom and Dad brought Lisa to me because they were worried about her temper. She does not explode at school but has at home. Yelling is not acceptable within their home.

I have been working with Lisa to help her understand and control her volcano (temper), teaching her how to handle life's inevitable mistakes. I point out all the wonderful traits I see in Lisa to both Lisa and her parents. Finally, I work with Lisa's parents to help her find acceptable outlets for her energy and temper. Lisa's parents expect her to be more like her sister. What is Lisa allowed to do with all that energy? Is there a place or way for her to release energy and it be all right within the home? Anger is just an emotion. We all get angry. It is important to learn what to do with anger. It is difficult to do that in a family where it seems no one but Lisa gets angry. Lisa and I discuss the fact that just as she learned to ride a bike, she needs to learn how to handle her anger. We brainstorm ideas from jumping up and down on a trampoline, to drawing, to tearing up old telephone books as physical releases for her anger.

Finally, Brianna presents an example of the middle of the protection channel.

> **Brianna: Learning Self-Limits**
>
> Brianna has been the tallest girl in her class throughout her life. She has had to learn self-discipline early; her size made her easily seen as a bully. As a three-year-old, if she ran past someone and the child fell, she might be accused of pushing the other child. Her mother and father have worked hard to help her learn how to handle her own body and emotions, to set her own limits.
>
> Brianna is now in fifth grade. Recently, her mother called me worried because of an incident at school. During gym class, Brianna had placed a piece of gum on the bench while she dressed. Another girl saw it, grabbed it, and said she was keeping it. Brianna told her it was hers and asked for it back. When the other girl would not give it back, Brianna tried to get it out of the other girl's hand. In the process, the other girl's little finger was fractured. Brianna was suspended from school for the remainder of the day. Nothing happened to the other girl.
>
> Now the other girl is demanding Brianna give her things in order to make up for "breaking" her finger. Brianna is a loving child who feels sad she hurt the other girl so she has given her gum, pencils, etc.

Mom called me to find out how to help Brianna. First, we talked about speaking with the principal about the fact that the girl who was stealing received no consequence for her actions. By no one recognizing her first action—stealing—she has taken on the role of victim and by doing so is now actually bullying Brianna. Brianna needed to learn how to handle herself and her own emotions when bullied. We also discussed how to respond to the bully.

Remember, protecting parents are not parents who prevent all harm to their child. Instead, by the time the child is in fifth grade, we protect by teaching and seeing if she is ready to run on her own. As the child grows, parents should see themselves as blocking linemen in football. We don't help our older children move forward by insisting they stay behind us as we stop all tacklers or bullies. Instead, we run in front and block until they become capable of running around us and scoring or handling issues for themselves.

How does protection change over time?

When navigating the channel of protection, in infancy, the parent supplies external limits that will help the child feel protected. By adulthood, these limits must be supplied internally by the adult child. Again, this is not a linear process. Notice the irregularity of the channel. This is a process of learning, with the child ultimately taking over the responsibility to protect himself.

Protection

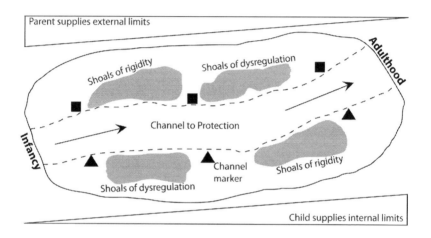

While on the journey of protection, the parent must be aware of the shoals. When limits are about power and are controlled solely by the parent, the child does not develop his own sense of internal limits. Depending upon the child's disposition, he can either rebel against the parents' external limits and end up on the shoals of dysregulation or he can become rigidly reliant upon such limits the rest of his life. In this latter case, the child will be unable to judge right from wrong using his own moral reasoning so he will use the substitute of rigid, externally supplied rules. The shoals on the other side of the channel are equally dangerous. A child who feels unprotected from the world and perhaps from his parents' emotions (they supply no limits even to themselves) could end up on the shoals of dysregulation. He may be unable to limit himself emotionally or to follow social or societal rules. On the other hand, a child without external limits may be forced to overcompensate and supply his own rigid, internal limits. Which shoal is reached depends upon the child's own temperament but the effects—either dysregulation or emotional rigidity—are equally dysfunctional.

What interferes with helping my child feel protected?

- *Fear that the child will be unhappy*

As stated earlier in the book, parents believe their child should be happy. It appears that many parents believe the child's happiness is the most important goal of parenting. However, by making happiness the number-one priority, we are teaching other lessons—entitlement, ingratitude, manipulativeness, and emotional dysregulation. These traits will not lead to happiness.

> **Janice and Bobby's Ingratitude**
> Janice (nine) and Bobby (seven) are visiting their grandparents. Grandpa and the whole clan have been invited to other relatives' cabin to play for the day. The clan arrives at lunch where the hosts have spread out a sumptuous buffet with ten to fifteen choices of food. Janice and Bobby take a look at all the choices and then go directly to their hostess and ask her to make them a peanut-butter-and-jelly sandwich. The hostess reported later, "I was shocked but did as I was asked."

Janice and Bobby had conveyed ingratitude to their hostess. She wondered aloud in my office if she should be honored that they could speak their minds with her or if she should be insulted. She questioned if it was okay for her to say, "No," and ask them to try the food she had been preparing for hours. She questioned whether she was hurting Janice and Bobby by not teaching them what is polite and impolite at other people's houses. Janice and Bobby need to understand the etiquette of being a guest in others' homes. If they are not taught these manners, they could be rejected by their friends' parents. Surely Janice and Bobby, if not instructed in basic manners, might come to feel rejected in the community but not understand why. They might come away believing they are simply not good enough to be accepted in other people's homes. All of this started because their parents wanted Janice and Bobby to be happy. The parents were afraid of saying no, of setting limits. They did not take the time to teach Janice and Bobby to appreciate what is offered.

Janice and Bobby were not taught gratitude by their parents. I often tell children in my office that when someone (e.g., Mom, Dad, Aunt, Grandma) prepares a meal, it is a gift of time and energy. It is impolite and not okay to refuse to try some. Children must learn to be gracious when receiving gifts. They do not need to try all foods but should attempt some and be thankful!

- ***Fear of conflict***

The fear of conflict with a child is rampant in parents today. Sometimes it is both parents, sometimes only one. In either case, the child learns some very unwelcome behaviors.

> **Aiesha's Rants**
> Aiesha is in third grade and hates homework. Aiesha's dad wants his daughter to be happy, and he hates conflict. She has learned to cry and complain until a parent virtually does all the work for her. Aiesha will say she doesn't want to do her homework; she'll rant that she never gets to play. Often, she will cry and whine that she is stupid. Dad has taken to giving her the answers in order to get through the homework fast and, he hopes, prevent her fits.

The biggest problem with this scenario, which all parents have experienced, is that Aiesha now believes that neither she nor Dad thinks she is capable of learning what is required in her homework. If she was capable, Dad wouldn't give her the answers.

What is Aiesha learning? She is learning that to get her way, she need only cry and complain and, best of all, put herself down. It seems to be working in the short term. However, if Aiesha succeeds, what will become of her? She will fall further and further behind her peers and eventually feel so incompetent she may drop out of school.

What else could her parents do? They must investigate what makes Aiesha feel incompetent. Children often tell me they feel stupid. Feeling stupid and being stupid are not the same. Have they had her learning tested? What is in the way of her learning? If she has a short attention span, can she learn that she works best in short segments, taking brief breaks? If she has a production problem (e.g., a problem writing, like dysgraphia, which means difficulty writing due to hand and finger problems), she can learn to use the computer, or until she has the keyboarding skills, she can dictate longer writings to her dad. Discovering what is in her way gives Aiesha's parents ideas about how to make her feel successful. This should not be used as an excuse to avoid the learning task, but as support for learning.

Note that the very reason for this conflict is that Dad does not like conflict; in fact, he is actually afraid of conflict. Dad needs to face this fear. It is causing him to essentially do Aiesha's homework for her, which in turn causes her to continue the struggle each day so he will continue to do her homework. He has forgotten the big-picture goal, which is to create a competent, caring, contributing adult. How can Aiesha become a confident adult if he does her work for her?

Dad must learn to think more like a soldier. As I learned indirectly through my U.S. Marine drill-instructor father, soldiers are afraid going into battle. They are given a mission by their superior officer, and they work as a team to perform this mission. It may be an incredibly difficult mission, but by maintaining focus on this mission, they can work through their fear to accomplish it.

All parents are afraid of one thing or another. As parents, we must not let fear of our child's unhappiness or our fear of conflict interfere with our mission. We must change our focus from our fear to our goals as parents. This helps us work through the battles that inevitably occur.

- **Feeling sorry for the child**

Feeling sorry for your child is one of the most destructive acts a parent can do. When parents feel sorry for their child, they often give her permission to avoid growing up, to avoid any responsibility for herself. This form of dysregulation does not lead to happiness but to discouragement and depression.

> **Joaquin's Irresponsibility**
>
> When Joaquin was in eighth grade, he entered a large public middle school. Joaquin was a brilliant young man who could talk for hours with any adult. However, he was not very good socially with his peer group. His awkwardness shone like a beacon attracting the school bullies. Joaquin was also very perfectionistic. In his brilliance, he would read volumes on any subject he was assigned but had extraordinary difficulty completing papers because his expectations were so high. By the second half of eighth grade, Joaquin began complaining about his stomach. It hurt, and he said he could not go to school. It was clear to all concerned that his stomach really hurt. However, all medical workups showed

no definitive cause. Joaquin missed more and more school. He believed he hurt too much to attend. His mother was caught between listening to how badly her son felt and believing he should be at school. After all, he didn't seem to feel that bad at home. Joaquin seemed to believe even the slightest symptoms (e.g., cold, sinus infection, stomachache) entitled him to avoid what was expected of him. He would stay home, read for hours, and play a computer game or two.

Although Joaquin started a new school in high school, he seemed to carry with him the idea that he could choose when he completed his assignments. Joaquin has struggled every summer to complete work not completed during the school year. Joaquin is now thinking about college, even though it terrifies him. Given his track record, he is afraid he will not be able to do his work. He is afraid to go into young adult life with all its expectations. Joaquin says he will only be a success if he becomes famous. Watching him is like watching a gambler waiting for the big win. In the meantime, he's too scared to accept the responsibilities of daily life.

In many families, Joaquin's stomach problems would have gone unnoticed. Staying home simply would not have been an option. However, Joaquin's mom listened and felt genuinely bad for her son, so she allowed him to stay home. However, what did Joaquin learn from all this? Adults are expected to complete their work, meet deadlines, ignore minor ailments, and function responsibly. Joaquin has learned to live in a world that does not exist for adults.

Mom's overprotection of Joaquin, albeit with loving intentions, has helped contribute to Joaquin's future of problems.

Are there rituals that can help my child feel protected?

Rituals of protection provide helpful limits to teach your child self-regulation. With a younger child they can be as simple as always asking him to take your hand to cross the street. As your child grows and attends school, rituals are more likely to be routines that demonstrate self-regulation. An example is the expectation that his homework is done before he watches television or plays games. By repeating this ritual daily you demonstrate work ethic: do your work before you play. After the work is done, each of you may check his backpack to be sure his is ready for the next day of school. This too is a ritual of protection. You do it with him until he does it on his own.

The routine of having a regular bedtime for your child, stopping what you are doing and helping your child get to bed, is also a ritual of protection. In your willingness to stop your life, you demonstrate self-regulation. In making sure he keeps a regular bedtime, you help protect him from the emotional dysregulation that can come from being overtired.

All families, at some point, place charts on the refrigerator. When your child is little, a chart may list the tasks he has to do before he leaves for daycare, e.g. dress, eat, brush his teeth, put shoes and coat on. As he gets older, the list may outline jobs he has to accomplish in order to get an allowance. These charts are a way to teach him what is expected of him within the family and, as these lessons are learned, what is expected of him in life. They represent boundaries or limits of what he must do. Without arguing, you as the parent provide a way for him to see the limits. Charts, if kept positive, can be a ritual of protection.

As your child begins to play at other children's homes, a ritual of protection involves your calling the parent at the home he will visit. You verify the parameters of the arrangement and the fact that an adult will be present. In this way when your child becomes a teenager and wants to attend a party, he will know you will telephone the parents of the person giving the party. Verification will have become a ritual.

I am sure you can think of many other rituals that serve to say to your child, "I protect you. I want you to make decisions that protect yourself as you grow."

What signs or channel markers let me know I'm still in the channel?

I stated in the security chapter that certain "sayings" are channel markers that keep us as parents within the channels of parenting with love. The following are some that I use to remind parents. You may certainly know others.

- ***Protection Channel Marker #1: Grown-ups take care of children; children don't take care of grown-ups.***

Nurture and caretaking flow downstream or down generations. Grandparents took care of the parents when they were children. Then parents take care of their children. Sometimes a parent may get sick and need help from their children. This is an exception, not the rule. Children need to participate in the work of the family, but this is little compared to the work of the parent. The work children are given needs to be age appropriate.

When a young child consistently and continuously takes care of her parent(s), this reversal takes a toll on her. She is left to handle problems that she knows are too big for her. Her parents are not protecting her with safe boundaries. In some families, this is necessary (e.g., a single mom may have a mental illness or a chronic physical disability). Besides gaining many skills associated with older children and adults, the child will experience a sense of distrust of adults, will lose the ability to know what she feels inside, and will sense that she has no support and has to handle the world by herself. Parents, by not setting limits upon themselves, can leave their child unprotected.

> **Savannah, The Parentified Child**
> Savannah is seven years old and the oldest of three daughters. Both her mother and father have drug addictions. Savannah can remember sitting on the lawn with her little sisters and a police officer while the other policemen searched her family's house. Because Mom and Dad were users, Savannah states factually she's good at taking care of her sisters. She can change a diaper. She can fix them all food when Mommy won't get up. Savannah states with pride, "I even know where to kick a man if he tries to hurt my sisters or me." The only problem is that Savannah doesn't know this is too much responsibility for a seven-year-old. She also doesn't trust any adult to take care of her or her sisters. She hoards food and steals.

Savannah's reactions are understandable. She's learned to protect herself. However, inside, she's frightened. She's afraid she's not lovable. If she were more lovable, if she were better, her mom and dad would have loved her. She trusts no one.

This is an extreme example. Others happen every day with parents who are sick. We have many children in America who come home from school and cook for their siblings and a parent who is ill. Some do this day after day. They have long days between work at home and work at school. Their schoolwork often falters.

Getting Back in the Channel:

Children need to know there are adults who are reliable and will be there to help them with the big, scary world. They need to know it's not their job to handle a world for which they are not prepared. As children grow, we need to teach them coping and problem-solving skills for this world.

If you are sick or overstressed one day and you ask your child to help, that is an exception. If your child cannot make school playdates, parties, etc., because he is doing an adult's work, other arrangements need to be made. Sometimes we can create a family if we are living isolated from other family members (e.g., two single moms living together, helping each other and their children). Find community and resources. Those resources are not just for your child but also for you. It is important to discern what is in the way of your protecting your child and subsequently helping him feel loved.

- ***Protection Channel Marker #2: Love unconditionally; do not accept unconditionally.***

During infancy, love is unconditional and feels less confusing than later in life. As humans begin to grow and assert themselves, they move in directions that parents may not like. At that point, although love may be unconditional, liking the behavior of the child is not unconditional. It may become confusing to the child when the parent sets limits. If you become angry or disappointed in a behavior, does that somehow mean you do not love your child? If you separate from her or separate her from the rest of the family, does this mean you don't love her? If, in adolescence, she goes somewhere in the car without your permission and you ground her, denying her the use of the family car, does this mean you do not love her? This marker is about learning, through love, how to not accept certain behavior. Later, we will talk about acceptance in love.

You can both love someone unconditionally and not accept his actions or your actions when you are with him. All healthy relationships involve some amount of boundary setting. Boundaries involve what we will and will not do in the context of the relationship. I have specialized in working with children who have poor boundaries. Boundaries are poor in these children because they are prone to sensory overload. They notice every sight, sound, smell, and texture in their environment. They often do not have the ability to focus on what is important in a situation because they cannot block the less important stimuli, the "noise." When they are little, they talk to parents nose to nose. They physically run into their parents, not quite realizing where their bodies stop and their parents' bodies begin. These children are born without a sense of boundaries. Parents are constantly helping them learn these boundaries. They teach them boundaries by giving them structure. Structure is a bedtime. Structure involves natural order, such as learning to put your snow pants on, then your boots, and then your mittens. It doesn't work well to put your boots on first and then try pulling your snow pants over them.

Boundaries also involve general respect rules for social relationships. You may not yell in someone's face. You may not hit another person. When a person violates those markers (e.g., hitting), you may still love that person, but you certainly don't like that behavior. If you do not communicate to the other person that she has violated your boundary, she has no way of knowing not to do it again. In parent-child relationships, parents are constantly helping children learn a sense of boundary about what they may or may not do in the relationship. Some children are very intense from birth and learn self-regulation through a loving parental relationship. They become adults who feel passionately and intensely, but do not beat other people up, hurt others, or expect others to regulate their emotions. Through boundaries offered in love, they learn to regulate their own emotions.

> **Mary's Grumpiness**
> Five-year-old Mary is tired. She has been grumpy all morning. Mom thinks she may have a cold. Anytime Mary has been asked to cooperate, she has reacted with a tirade. Mom explains to Mary that she needs to have a rest in the afternoon. She loves Mary, but Mary has had little ability to be a family helper. Mary and Mom take a time-out from each other at 2:00 PM. Mom explains she needs a break from the grumpiness. Mary can go to her room and nap or play quietly, but Mom needs to rest. She reiterates to Mary that at 2:30, the two of them can start again and the rest of the day can be better.

Mom accepts that Mary sometimes wakes up in a negative mood and often needs a fresh start once stuck in that mood. She does not need to berate Mary for her mood. This is much like the four-mistakes-a-day rule. Mom does, however, not have to accept the mood and rightly chooses to set a limit on not cooperating.

> **Charlie's Debt**
> Sixteen-year-old Charlie asks his mother for fifty dollars. She asks what it's for. It seems Charlie has borrowed the money from his friend, Max, to get tickets to a rock concert. Charlie wants his Mom to help him get out of debt with Max. Mom states she is sorry, but she will not give him the money. Charlie believes that not bailing him out means she does not love or support him.

Mom lets Charlie know that she loves him but doesn't want to support him in spending money he doesn't have. She loves him enough to support his bearing the consequences of his own decision—borrowing money. She asks him if he knows what he can do to earn the money by working at home for her. Once he does the work, she will be happy to pay him. In this way, Mom, besides expressing her love, lets Charlie know she does not accept his choice.

Getting Back in the Channel:

In the cases above, a solution was reached when the parents discussed the problem in the context of loving the other person. Letting a loved one know you love him but don't like what he is doing is a beginning. The two people then need to be open to all possible solutions. The answer is often surprising and cannot be only one person's view of an answer. In my office, children often come up with better solutions than I could have possibly imagined.

- **Protection Channel Marker #3: Love is not all or nothing.**

There is no person on the earth for whom we have loving feelings all the time. Everyone is human. There are things we like about our loved ones and things we don't like. As our beautiful baby grows, we come face-to-face with how that baby fits into the idea of our dream baby.

If the perfect baby slept through the night and ours doesn't, we begin the process of acceptance—accepting who this little person really is. In all loving relationships, we have to move from an idealization or honeymoon phase, where the person is perfect and does little wrong, to an acceptance of their real human flaws. Love is not all or nothing. Love is seeing all the human flaws of your loved ones and loving them anyway. Your child may be stubborn. You choose to view that stubbornness as persistence and help him learn where persistence helps him get his way and where it hurts him. Every strength has a weak side. Every weakness also presents a strength in some arena. If you place a person on a pedestal or idolize what love is, you will eventually become disillusioned with the loved one. Love is based in reality; idealization in fantasy. Again, love is not all or nothing. We must learn to accept who the other person really is.

The trick in the middle of acceptance is to know how far acceptance goes. When do we have to say, "I love you, but this behavior won't work for me." We discussed this earlier when we talked about not accepting unconditionally. Where is the balance? Most people would agree that you cannot accept poor behavior from someone else to the point that you are not taking care of yourself. For instance, you cannot allow someone to hit you. If you do, you teach them to value themselves above all others—to believe others are not worthy of respect.

The key to finding this balance between all or nothing is in holding both self-respect and other-respect in equal portions in a relationship. Other-respect cannot outweigh self-respect. Self-respect cannot be more important than other-respect. In accepting the other's flaws, are you somehow disrespecting yourself? In most cases, accepting another is letting go of the dream or expectations so you can build a new relationship based upon reality. But the new reality must be a place where both individuals are respected. If it is not, then the dream becomes a nightmare. Rules for relationships are mutual. They involve mutual give and take that comes from a place of mutual respect.

Every once in a while, I will get parents in my office who tell me their five- or six-year-old is out of control. They describe scenes in which the parents are being hit, kicked, or bitten. The parents say they do not believe in physical punishment and have never spanked or hit their child. They say they have told their child to stop and that it hurts. What is wrong with this picture?

Some of the time, such a child has a clinical problem and needs treatment, perhaps even medication. However, sometimes, the parents realize they are "marshmallows" in the way they set boundaries or limits. They say "no," but in a voice that is helpless. They learn when they say "no" firmly, not yelling, and are willing to back up their "no" by disengaging or stepping away from the child, they make a clear statement. When they remain with the child, the child mistakes their presence for permission to hit them. In walking away, the parents nonverbally state they will not remain to be hit either physically or verbally. Parents need to clearly communicate that they will be present as soon as the child is ready to talk about the problem.

In adulthood, most of us have known a relationship where someone is constantly putting us down, raging at us, or blaming us for his own problems. This person may be a friend, a co-worker, or a family member. Learning to set limits on such a relationship is a difficult and painful process. One adult cannot be responsible for another adult's happiness. The process of being with someone, especially a family member who is constantly demeaning you, causes some people to become depressed. Learning to say to these people that you care but there are limits is a growth step. Relationships need to feed us not drain us.

I use the same idea in parent-child relationships. Simply put, 90 percent of the interactions need to be positive and supportive so that the 10 percent of the interactions that involve teaching, coaching, or honesty and insight can be laid upon a positive foundation. No one, child or parent, can hear important feedback if she doesn't feel loved, cared about, and supported.

> **Kris's Terrible Day**
> Dad decided he wanted a special afternoon with his seven-year-old daughter, Kris. He took Kris to lunch, and then they went roller-skating together. As they were leaving the roller rink, Kris saw a toy on the counter and asked Dad if she could get it. Dad said, "No. We need to leave." Kris began to cry and say she had had a terrible day. Dad was devastated.

Clearly, Kris seemed to need more and more to make the day "good." When she had finally been told "no," the day was then "bad." Dad needed to help Kris see what she had received during the day (i.e., lunch and roller-skating with Dad alone). Then Dad could help her learn days are not all good or all bad. It was disappointing that she couldn't have the toy, but lunch and roller-skating were fun. Dad needed to understand that Kris and he had a wonderful time together for most of the day and just because she threw a fit at the end of it did not make the whole day bad for him. Days are not all or nothing, and neither is love.

Getting Back in the Channel:

Our children are not perfect. They are simply human. There are things they remember and things they forget. We can choose to live in a fantasy world where everything meets our expectations, or we can choose to live in the real world. In the real world, we have to learn to recognize what we are grateful for and what we have. We ultimately need to decide if what we have is enough, using reality as a filter.

- **Protection Channel Marker #4: Don't be a doormat; be a door.**

People walk past doormats by walking on them. A door, however, has the option of being open or closed. To love someone is to be neither a victim nor a perpetrator. It feels just as bad inside to be the person who walks upon others as it does to be the person walked upon. Neither is healthy. Love is being respectful of both yourself and others.

If you wish to raise children who respect others, you must respect your children. "Then why are there so many disrespectful children?" you ask. Many of these children have been treated disrespectfully. However, in today's society, I have seen another breed— a child for whom the mother and the father would never think of setting limits. They are doormats. In trying to be aware of their child's feelings, they are constantly disowning their own feelings.

The child grows up believing he is to be respected at all costs. He has no clue how rude and disrespectful he is to others. He grows up entitled. He is constantly aware of the things others do to offend him or slight him. He has no awareness of his responsibility to perform a dance of mutual respect.

If you are a door, when a child or adult begins screaming at you, you close the door. You reopen the door when you can talk about what frightened her, frustrated her, or made her angry.

If you are a door, you decide whether the door needs to be open or closed. If closed, how far?

If you are a doormat, after a while, you get tired and angry. You blow up in frustration or complain and whine about who is doing what to you. As a door, you recognize you have more choices in your openness or closedness. A parent sometimes shuts the door briefly to get a break in order to recuperate, take a breath, and decide what to do next. In that way, when you, the parent, speak about your child, it is with love, not anger and not to complain.

This principle of being a door, not a doormat applies in all loving relationships. We teach others to respect us when we respect ourselves. When we disrespect ourselves, we teach others to disrespect us. We disrespect ourselves when we allow other people to walk on us. They walk on us when we do not say no, when we do too much for them, when we do things for others they could do for themselves, or when we ask for nothing in return—not even a thank-you. Others walk on us when we don't have limits on what disrespect we will accept.

As for the people allowed to walk upon us, it is not healthy for them to believe there is a person who is responsible for meeting their needs. As we grow, we become more and more capable of and responsible for meeting our own needs. Others can help, but they cannot solve our problems for us. They are neither responsible for us, nor are they to blame when our needs are not met.

The last time developmentally that children can redo the assumptions of entitlement, responsibility, and blame is adolescence. Teenagers often try to blame their parents for their lives. They try to make their parents responsible for their misery by blaming their parents for the life choices the parents have made, like not saving enough for their college education or not buying them a car to drive to high school. It is only after they have left behind the entitlement and blame of others that they begin to show the maturity of young adulthood. They begin to see what their parents have given them and solve the problems of what they need to do to attain what they want and become who they want to be.

Unfortunately, oftentimes, adults you love have not finished this piece of work for themselves. You do them no service by playing the role of caretaker; you thus implicitly agree that they are right. By right, I mean that they are correct in assuming that you are responsible for them, that they are entitled to your energy and resources, and that you are to blame for their failures. Needless to say, a person cannot continue to grow and develop while holding on to such assumptions. When you begin to set limits and boundaries, you state that you do not agree with such unhealthy assumptions.

> **Peter's Complaints**
> Peter's grandmother has had enough! She watches eight-year-old Peter before and after school. Lately, she or Peter ends up calling Peter's mom two or three times during their time together. Grandma has never been able to say no to Peter. Peter now constantly complains to Grandma. She is supposed to take him toy shopping when he wants, rent a video when he wants, or let him have friends over when he chooses. Either Grandma is constantly complaining to Mom about Peter, or Peter is complaining about Grandma to Mom.

Mom tells Peter, "Staying with Grandma is a privilege, because she will let you do things, like have your best friend over and other things that you would not be able to do if you were in day care." She again reiterates to Grandma that she has to say, "No," to Peter and stick to it. Peter has learned she will give in if he's rude or whiny. Grandma has been a doormat for Peter for too long.

> **Tanya's "Sorry" Card**
> Tanya is the apple of her father's eye. He does not seem to be capable of saying "No" to her. Despite her behavior, he gives her whatever she wants. If she needs money, he gives it to her. Mom is frustrated and has simply stopped trying to talk to Dad about his behavior. She believes it does no good because Dad can't seem to say, "No." Tanya calls Dad and tells him to go buy prom tickets for her and her date at the high school. She pleads that she is "too busy." Dad leaves work and goes to buy the tickets because he feels sorry for Tanya. He notices he is the only parent in the line. He believes her boyfriend is a jerk who mistreats her. Dad is conflicted because he doesn't want her to miss the experience of prom.

Remember the destructiveness of feeling sorry for your child. Once she gets it into her head that she can get her way by playing that card, she will play it all the time. She may even intentionally exhibit destructive behaviors like choosing an abusive boyfriend to have enough "sorry" cards in her hand. Being a door means you can say "No" (be closed) when the "sorry" card is played and be open when it is not.

Getting Back in the Channel:

By not exercising a modicum of self-respect in either of the previous examples, Grandma and Dad have not helped teach the people they love how to respect themselves or others. Tanya is already involved in an abusive relationship at seventeen. By saying, "Stop, you cannot continue this way!" you demonstrate self-respect to the people you love. People who act as doormats often have no awareness of this behavior. They are not present to or aware of their feeling of being used. It is as if they give away all the respect they wish to have for themselves. Until they get present or become aware of their own feelings and begin to see this interaction, they cannot stop.

Learning to balance self-respect and other-respect requires exercising both sides of this equation simultaneously. Too much emphasis on one or the other leads to unhealthy relationships. Remember, don't be a doormat; be a door.

- **Protection Channel Marker #5: Good things come to those who wait.**

Waiting is a form of self-discipline; it is a limit. By learning to delay self-gratification, kids learn to decenter (i.e., to not have to be the center of attention, to stop and think before acting on an impulse, and to understand the beginnings of a work ethic). All these pieces are valuable lessons for your child. Each of these lessons will add to an adult becoming competent, caring, and contributing.

This channel marker can be started early with your child. Offer to let him choose a treat if he can stay in the cart and be helpful while grocery shopping. The treat may be chewing gum or, as in my children's case, a muffin or doughnut.

Recognizing the limits of your child's development, unique temperament, and health is important to success. Asking a two- or three-year-old when she is well rested and healthy to make a thirty- to forty-five-minute grocery shopping excursion is conceivable. A two-hour grocery-shopping outing is not.

Too often, parents will buy their children something to stop them from complaining. This actually reinforces their complaining behavior. In a more constructive scenario, children are told how long they have to wait. If they successfully do so without too much complaint, a treat will reinforce this much more desirable behavior.

> **Trudy's Patience**
> Trudy was seven, and her grandmother was getting married. Trudy's mom got her up and made sure she was in her special dress three hours before the wedding. They all went to the church to take pictures and set up. Trudy came along. Trudy behaved beautifully at the wedding. However, as the time ticked on, they left the church and went to another building for the reception. An hour into the reception, the entire room heard Dad yelling at Trudy from the kitchen. "Trudy, go out there and behave. If you don't, I'm going to give you a spanking." (She had been running around the reception room.)

Trudy had been in her party dress for over five hours. She had behaved beautifully. Where are the good things that come to those who wait in the above example? Children learn the most from positive reinforcement, not from being threatened or from physical pain. Had I been asked, I would have suggested only being at the wedding thirty minutes or at most an hour before it began. I probably would have encouraged letting her run around to let off some steam before the reception as well as leaving earlier rather than later. Instead, Trudy was not rewarded for all her good behavior but shamed and punished for her indiscretion.

HOW DO I BEGIN AND CONTINUE THE JOURNEY TO PROTECTION?

Getting Back in the Channel:

If you are constantly complaining and yelling about what your child does wrong, stop. Your child is getting all your energy for misbehaving. Start putting your energy toward behavior you want, not the behavior you don't want. That energy comes in many forms:
1) excitement, joy, the tone of your voice;
2) time and attention from you, doing something special together; and
3) token payoffs or rewards, such as muffins, gaining more media time, or even on occasion buying a toy the child really wants.

Can protection be lost and regained?

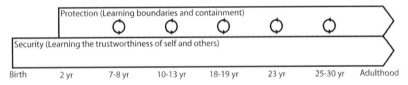

In the security chapter, I talked about how trust of other and trust of self is constantly renegotiated. The same is true of protection. As children approach age two, they test your limits. "All by self" is a common phrase. They test how far they can go with you and still have your protection.

Will you protect me in preschool if another child is mean? Will you protect me from myself, my own ideas, my own willfulness? What will you do if I get homework in kindergarten and scribble all over it because I do not wish to do it? Will you protect me from bullies in junior high school? Will you teach me how to protect myself? Again, the circles represent normal times when the child revisits the questions: Will you protect me? Am I capable of protecting myself? These circular flow symbols do not represent the only times the issue of protection is renegotiated; other times can be triggered by the illness or death of a sibling or parent, moving, the divorce of parents, the loss of the first love, etc.

> **Brian Renegotiates Protection**
> Brian is in tenth grade at a boarding high school. This is his first year at this school. For the last three years, he was in a boarding middle school. His first love is in ninth grade at the old boarding school. Her parents have decided she should break up with Brian now since he is not in school with her any longer. The parents have told her school not to allow any contact between her and Brian.
> Brian is devastated. He calls his mother and says, "Mom, remember when I was in second grade and there was that teacher who was mean to me? You talked to the principal and made it all better. You promised me then that you would always protect me. I need your protection now." Brian is aware his mother is a powerful attorney who can be very aggressive. He wants her to be aggressive now with his girlfriend's parents.

Brian's mom instead says she believes it was wrong of his girlfriend's parents to interfere with the two of them. She does not want to be like his girlfriend's mom and interfere between the couple, so she chooses not to call his girlfriend's mother. She offers to be there for him and help in any other way but believes that kind of interference at this age would be inappropriate. This is part of growing, and it hurts. She loves her son but recognizes the limits of that love. It is now time for him to handle his own love relationship. She does not believe any parent should interfere unless the child's safety is involved.

Setting limits on yourself and what you will do to protect your child may be just as difficult as setting limits on her when she is younger. Understanding that handing off this responsibility will make your child a more responsible adult can help ease such difficulties.

Conclusion

How do I help my child feel protected? After we have established a relationship with our child by being trustworthy, we become our child's teacher. It is our job to teach him how to belong in our society. Children want to belong. We do him no service when we do not teach him what the limits of his behavior are. Children who hurt others will not be liked by their peers. Some children do not have any idea how their behavior affects their peers. Most children, whether they hit, call names, or cry, just want to belong.

As parents, it is our job to teach our children the rules of belonging. This can be done in a loving way. The first time or two you can simply say, "There's a secret no one has told you: [then the lesson] you can't hit your friends or they will not want to play with you," etc. The child needs to know you believe in him and his ability to abide by the limits or boundaries about which you are instructing him. He needs to know you will be there for him as he learns. He can make mistakes, but he will get better and better at handling his body and his emotions. You will notice and celebrate each step.

CHAPTER 4

What Is Important about Feeling Important?

All children want to belong. Belonging starts when the child feels secure and protected. However, when she feels important to you, her sense of belonging grows. Her importance can be demonstrated through your words, but your actions speak louder than words. When you come home, do you stop and spend time finding out how her day has gone? Do you go straight to your computer without stopping to connect to her? Do you listen to her when she speaks? Or, is she so important she can interrupt you at any time; you never do anything for yourself; you praise her despite her own behavior? Being somewhere between these examples allows you to help her gain true esteem.

What does importance look like within my child's and my relationship?

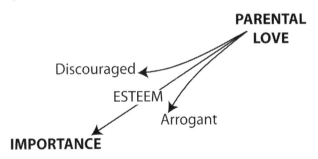

As a preschooler, your child learns to take initiative. She has a good idea and tries to imitate adults in her world. She moves forward with a purpose in life. The child feels importance from her parents. She believes she will have enough good ideas to go into the world. Her learning, her growth is important to you.

As children continue to grow, they will have many "good ideas" about the world and how to be in the world. These ideas need to be seen as a great way to help that child feel important. Children have great ideas; however, there are times when those ideas won't work. She should not have everything she wants. Some parents mistake importance for overindulgence, buying her everything they think she wants. Remember, children gain a sense of importance when their thinking is honored. Honoring does not mean saying "yes" all the time to their wishes, desires, and whims. They have some "great" ideas, and some that will simply not work or be socially acceptable. She may be very smart, but if she insists on changing the rules of a game with her friends, she may not have friends for long. The balance is toward importance, but not without some recognition of others. In this way, we teach her she is important but so are others and their ideas. We learn lessons each day to notice what we have, not what we do not have. We as parents work to determine what is her deepest desire and what is just a whim. A part of our work is to let her know that what is important to her is important to us. We demonstrate importance when we share in her passions or interests. If a child feels unimportant, it is easy to think that the way to belong is by having those around her treat her as if she is important. If a child feels unimportant, she may constantly try to put others in her service to try to feel important. Having other people wait on you is not a healthy way to be important. In fact, the outcome is not the development of true esteem but rather a constant craving for attention. This attention-seeking may come in the form of drama (e.g., rage or a victim story), which engages other family members but does not increase esteem.

Remember, to feel important, there must be a balance in the feedback you give a child. He may be a naturally good athlete, but if his goal is to be in the NBA, he needs to know the work involved in reaching his goal. An article in the February 2008 issue of *Mother Jones* stated that 85 percent of parents think it is important to regularly tell their kids they are smart. When researchers asked four hundred fifth-graders to complete a puzzle, 90 percent of those praised for effort picked a harder puzzle the next time. A majority of those praised for being smart chose an easier puzzle the next time. Kids who are too often reminded that they are smart tend to sidestep challenges in order to avoid any evidence that they may not be smarter than others. They are afraid to be tested and come up short.

In the next examples, please note that Jacob struggles with the discouraged side of the channel, Kristen struggles with the arrogance side, and Emma and her dad find their way to the middle of the importance channel.

Jacob's Discouragement

Jacob, as Mom puts it, has always had to do things in his own way, in his own time. Mom and Dad have worried about Jacob his whole life—Mom more than Dad. Although Jacob is a brilliant sixteen-year-old, he has had a difficult time getting his assignments handed in to his teachers in a timely manner. It's as if deadlines do not exist for him. Through the years, his parents have tried everything (e.g., depriving him of media time), but if Jacob doesn't want to work, he just won't. He's very content to just read for hours and hours. His parents and teachers all agree he is intelligent. Jacob will read about a topic voraciously, learn a great deal, and then stop—he just won't write the paper and finish it.

> Jacob wants to do something important with his life. He wants to be famous for his life's work. However, he does not practice the self-discipline necessary to finish his schoolwork. Jacob's parents tell him how bright he is. Jacob seems terrified he cannot do anything right for Mom. He believes she will not accept him for what he likes or wants, only what she believes is important. Jacob's mother feels like a complete failure. Her life has been the raising of her children. It is important to her that he does his work. Jacob will work as long as his father works with him. However, his father is often not available. Jacob is good socially with adults but does show signs of depression and Asperger's syndrome.

Jacob wants to work but is afraid his work will not meet expectations. Mom tries to show Jacob he is important by packing his lunch and doing his laundry. Jacob is a senior this year. Mom is afraid to let him go. Jacob is mad at her and wants to leave but is terrified he will not be able to fulfill his dreams. He clearly feels inferior and frozen in fear. Mom also feels as if she has failed.

Although Jacob is likely biologically predisposed to depression, this mental state has been reinforced by his being the center of attention for his parents, especially his mom. He feels he must be worth this attention, but then he realizes he has not deserved it. He has big dreams that when they come to fruition mean he will deserve attention from a wider audience, but then he realizes that he is not capable of anything. Because of this, he fluctuates between arrogance, expecting to be waited on, and discouragement.

Jacob's expectation of importance is too high. He has not decentered his attention from solely being on himself; he assigns little importance to others. Neither the caring, the competent, nor the contributing parts of the parenting goal will be achieved until he does.

> **Emma's Story: Importance Means Follow-Through**
>
> Dad loves his daughter Emma, age ten. He and Mom have been divorced for over four years. Dad feels a great loss since he did not want the divorce. Not only did he lose his wife, but now Emma doesn't want to be at his house. Dad is stuck, constantly blaming Mom for Emma's reticence to be with him on the weekend. He believes Mom says bad things about him to Emma. Even if she doesn't, he sees Mom roll her eyes at him in front of Emma. Dad is often in a competition with Mom about who can be the better parent, for instance, who lets her have her friends for sleepovers more, watch television, etc. He knows Mom was her primary parent for many years before the divorce. Now he wants time and involvement with Emma.
>
> Emma comes to me and is clear—she does not believe she is important to Dad. When she is at Dad's, he sometimes leaves her with sitters. What she doesn't say is that to Dad's credit, he gets a sitter she knows well. What she does say is, "I have little time with him, and then he leaves me." Her experience of Dad is, "He is always telling me what I am going to do when I am with him." It is her belief he does not hear her and what she likes or wants. For instance, he tells her she has to ride her bike and does not listen to what she would rather do outside.

In the office, I helped Dad look at what importance means to children. Importance in parenting is listening to your child's good ideas, allowing the child to initiate and to have ideas, and then validating those ideas. Not all ideas need to be acted upon by the parent. Some ideas really won't work because of time constraints, finances, etc. However, make sure the child is validated enough to feel important. Part of Dad's dilemma is in listening to what outsiders say is right or wrong. Dad wants to be a good parent. However, in listening to other adults' ideas, he is not listening to Emma. Instead of hearing her, he is competing with Mom about who is right or who is the best parent. A way to show importance might be to play a game with Emma that she likes and have a conversation with her exploring what is good and bad about it. That way, the focus is not on who is the best parent but instead on teaching the child your values and helping her to feel important.

After a session with Dad talking about importance, Dad called and reported that the last weekend with Emma was fabulous. Dad had worked on listening to her. He no longer was stuck on looking like the best parent but was trying to hear Emma and work with her to create a relationship. In church that weekend, she was squirmy. In the past, he said, he would have just been irritated and expected her to behave. However, this time, he whispered if she could sit still, they would stop by the doughnut shop afterward. Then, as he put it, "After church, I remembered to do it. Usually, I'd forget."

Kristen's Arrogance

Kristen is nineteen years old. She is the older sister of a sixteen-year-old brother. Kristen's mother is divorced and has devoted herself to raising her two children, praising them for everything they did. Both children have attended a small parochial school. Kristen's graduating class had only twenty-three other students.

> Kristen has always enjoyed singing and performing. In her small school, she received many of the lead roles in the musical productions. She also sang in the choir at her church. Kristen decided to go to a small college nearby and major in music. She dropped out after one semester, saying she thought it was a waste of time. She didn't want to take voice lessons or study music theory; she thought she knew everything she needed to know about these things already. Kristen convinced her mother to pay a local recording studio to help her record a CD. She did not recognize how much training she needed or the competitiveness of the music industry. The CD sold about as well as you would expect from a teenager with little talent but with a high opinion of herself: no sales at all.

The result of this fiasco was that Kristen eventually went back to college. Her life has changed course; she no longer sees herself as the center of everyone's universe. However, it took a hard and expensive lesson before she could see herself in the context of the wider world.

How does importance change over time?

Within the channel of importance, a child who is treated as unimportant inevitably, under the strain of the world, becomes discouraged. Whereas others who are allowed to believe they are too important develop a false bravado and become arrogant, treating others as unimportant. Their parents do not ask their children to treat them as important, and these children continue to diminish the importance of other people long into adulthood.

In early childhood, at the start of the channel of importance, the parent is the major supplier of esteem to the child. Each day, the parent demonstrates the joy this child brings to his life. As the child grows and enters the larger world, she listens to all that is around her and discerns for herself her true esteem. This channel involves the child learning that she may be the sun within her own family, but she is but one star in the galaxy of the larger world. By the end of this journey of growth, the child must attain her own sense of importance and esteem. In adulthood, we cannot expect the world to supply esteem to us. We must carry a sense of true esteem within ourselves as we go through the ups and downs of life.

If the parent grants the child too much importance, she can become stranded on the shoals of arrogance. She may believe her talent, beauty, intelligence, or skill to be better than any other because that is what her parents unintentionally led her to believe. On the other side of the channel are the shoals of discouragement. Here, her parents may have ignored her and not noticed her talents, intelligence, etc. They may have seen other children as talented instead of their own child, or they may have focused more upon themselves.

Importance

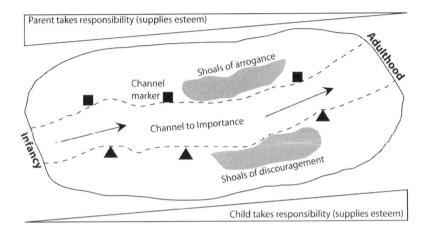

What interferes with my child feeling an appropriate level of importance?

Most of us want our child to know she is important to us. However sometimes, life takes over. Some parents become alcohol or drug or work addicted. They communicate that the only truly important thing is the next drink or the next high or the next work project. Far more parents simply become too busy with their own lives. They seem to forget there will only be a limited number of soccer games and years of childhood events. We are with our children a relatively short period of our lifetimes. Parents forget that the child may simply give up hoping they will be seen as important by the parent. On the other side of the channel is the child whom the parent sees as too important. The child's success becomes the parent's success. The parent's identity becomes fused with their own child's.

Being too busy

In her book *How Much Is Enough?* Jean Illsley-Clarke argues that parents simply don't want to take the time to teach their child. There are many reasons for this. Many parents are too busy; some can only be described as lazy. Some just hope their children will learn it on their own—by osmosis. They may fear they do not have the skills necessary to be a good parent so they don't try.

A good example of this is Emma's dad in an earlier story. Dad had been very busy working in his occupation and learning about parenting. However, he had failed to stop and be in the present moment with Emma. Parents may see unwanted consequences if they are too busy to pay attention to their children.

> **Colin's Bid for Attention**
> Colin is a five-year-old with a three-year old brother. His mom comes home from work before Dad. The childrens' nanny knows what will happen next. While she is with the boys, they are well behaved because she gives them the attention and the balanced sense of importance of self and other that they need. Colin knows, however, that, while his mom may have come home, her mind is either still back at work or is thinking of quickly getting on Facebook. Mom has no time for him. Until the nanny leaves, Colin stands near his younger brother waiting. As soon as the door closes, he hits his brother and the screaming begins.

Not all children will patiently wait for the feeling of importance that parents can give their child. If no effort is made by the parent to acknowledge this need, too often, the child will try to extract attention from the parent by potentially self- or other-destructive behavior.

Being too self-absorbed

Colin's mom is busy. She is also absorbed in pursuits other than parenting. Other parents may be absorbed in their own emotions.

> **Fiona's in the Middle**
> Fiona, who is in second grade, has a brother in fifth grade. Mom and Dad are divorced and don't get along. She tells the children that because she does not have them for either Christmas Eve or Christmas this year that there will be no Christmas in her house. They feel like they are being punished for being with their dad as the court has ordered. They are devastated.

Mom says she sees no reason to buy presents or put up a tree before they leave for Dad's house. I explain she does not have to compete with Dad. She doesn't have to spend much but not getting any presents at all tells her children that they are not important to her. Mom is so absorbed with her own loss that she fails to even begin to comprehend how her choice affects her children.

Fears and anxieties as parents

Parents who place too much importance on the child are often doing so because they place too much importance on looking good, being needed, on not letting go of their child, etc. In some ways, it is also a sign of self-absorbance. The parents are not aware of what their children need, but are driven by their own fears and anxieties.

> **Katie's Story**
> Twenty-two-year-old Katie says she "cannot boil water." She describes herself as having grown up in a middle-class family with a mom who stayed home to raise her children. Mom thought her role was to do everything for her children. She still does Katie's laundry. Her mother worried that Katie would make a mess in the kitchen. Her kitchen had to be spotless. "My boyfriend knows how to cook, so I just don't bother trying anymore."

Remember Bruce who just gave up and didn't take his exams or Jacob who never seemed to get anything accomplished? How could their parents have encouraged them to grow? Their parents could have allowed their children opportunities to solve problems themselves. Both moms unintentionally did too much. Did they do too much for their children because of their children's fear or their own? Many parents want to be there for their children in ways they did not feel their parents were there for them. Some parents fear their child is not capable and subsequently make them less capable. Some parents are just afraid of not being needed by their child. Finally, others want the child to feel important and end up doing too much. It is difficult, but parents need to examine their own motivations for what they do.

WHAT IS IMPORTANT ABOUT FEELING IMPORTANT?

Bruce, Jacob, and Katie have something in common. They all have overly fearful parents who have kept them from growing up. The parents were absorbed with their own fears and unintentionally failed to help their children grow.

Listening too well: codependent parents

Not long ago on the *Oprah Winfrey Show*, Oprah interviewed a father who had quit his job to train his twelve-year-old son to become a professional football player. They had a strict regimen working out before and after school. Dad had taken a job delivering pizzas at times when his son was not in training. Who really had the most at stake in the boy becoming a professional athlete? At twelve, his son may have stated it was his goal, but the father clearly had tied too much of his own identity to this star. From his son's perspective, what is he learning from his father about being male and a husband and a father? What happens to the father if his son decides upon a different goal in a few years? What happens to the father if his son reaches his goal?

Another example of a parent who, out of love, unintentionally does too much for her child and too little for herself is Hannah's mother.

> **Hannah's Story**
> Hannah is twenty years old and a sophomore at a university in the same city in which she grew up. Hannah's mother calls and asks me to see Hannah. Her mother believes she has low self-esteem and low self-confidence. Mother reports that Hannah is too dependent upon her boyfriend. He is not abusive but does not treat her well. When I see Hannah, it is clear she is mad at her mother for interfering in her love life. Hannah believes the biggest problem is that her mother is too interfering. When I speak with Mom, I discover that she grew up in a home where she had

THE JOURNEY OF PARENTING

> too much responsibility as a child. She was expected to call her father for child support payments as a nine-year-old. Mom is overreacting to her own childhood lack of nurturance and support by providing for Hannah support she was not given as a child. She still does Hannah's laundry. Hannah calls her mother two to three times a day. Often, Hannah asks her Mom to pick up milk or a prescription and bring it to her at school or work. Mom has been overfunctioning in relation to Hannah throughout Hannah's life. Consequently, Hannah is not confident in herself and her abilities. She is overly dependent upon her mother and mad about it. Hannah's mother has done too much for her, thus creating unhealthy dependency. Hannah has transferred this dependence onto her boyfriend.

In the two stories of the pizza-delivering dad and Hannah's mom, the child's identity and happiness become too important to the parent. Children and parents are happiest when the other's importance is in balance with the self's importance.

The helicopter parent, like Hannah's mom, often has both issues of overprotectiveness and a need to make her child too important in her life. This in turn can lead to both dependency and discouragement for the child.

Can importance be lost and regained?

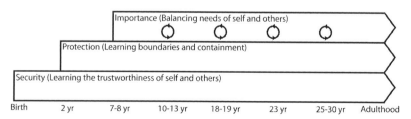

WHAT IS IMPORTANT ABOUT FEELING IMPORTANT?

As with security and protection, importance is gained, then questioned, maybe lost, and maybe regained. Security, protection, importance, and respect can be thought of as a bowl. Is it empty? Did a life experience add to the bowl? Did it take away from what you had already collected in the bowl?

There are many things that help fill the bowl of importance. Having your parents stop their lives and demonstrate your importance (e.g., attend your soccer game) fills your bowl. When your mom or dad misses your special "spoken word" performance, it subtracts from the bowl.

However, there are life factors over which we have little control that may dramatically add to or subtract from your child's bowl. The addition of a sibling, depending upon how it's handled, can add to or subtract from the other sibling's importance. During a divorce, parents are overwhelmed by loss and grief. During this time, the child's bowl may become emptier. However, I have seen some parents make the child too important. The mother or father may use the child as a confidante, as the "man of the house." On the outside, it may seem the parent is making the child more important. In reality, it is a selfish act whose effect is to diminish the importance of the child. The child at some level recognizes it is developmentally inappropriate. He may feel trapped between his parents in a role he knows he cannot perform.

Importance is learning to balance the needs of self and others. As we begin school, we discover that although we are wonderful in our parents' eyes, we are one of many in our classroom. We discover we may be good in math and running, but others are better readers. As we move into adolescence, we see that some friends date and others don't. Do any of these things make us more or less important?

On my first day of college, the dean made a speech. He said although some of my classmates' parents were doctors, judges, etc., that now made no difference. He stated that our importance in college and in life would be based upon our work and our participation in the college community.

People spend their entire lives working on the balance of importance with self and others. Certainly marriage and parenthood cause a shift in how full those bowls are. None of us want to be considered selfish, yet some of us are. Some of us work so hard at trying to help others feel important that we actually need to develop a sense of self-importance or self-care.

Are there rituals that can help my child feel important?

Rituals do not need to be elaborate to be effective. In fact, often the most effective are the simplest ones. Later in life, your children may amaze you with what rituals they remember and cherish.

One child I know talks about the last fifteen minutes of her day. Her mother always comes into her bedroom, and they talk. It is their time. She has three brothers and sisters. Mom or Dad reads to her each evening. Then the bedtimes are staggered. Mom time is the last ten to fifteen minutes of the day when each child gets time alone with Mom. They may discuss the day, dreams, worries, etc., but it is their time with Mom.

Another family I know, in which both parents worked, always had teatime with their children as they came home from work. As the mother explained, the tradition started because everyone was starving at the end of the day. They were starving for attention. At teatime, they all sat together and discussed their days with a small snack. When they were finished, homework could be done in the kitchen while parents set about preparing the evening meal. The mother said it never worked to go straight to meal preparation. According to her, she could either have teatime and everyone have a positive time or her children would grump and fight while she cooked.

WHAT IS IMPORTANT ABOUT FEELING IMPORTANT?

One father I know is always joking around with his older children, not in a way that puts anyone down, but in an inclusive way. For a while, he joked that they should all move to Santa Fe from snowy Minnesota. His daughters knew it was a joke and saw it as something they had between them, a shared experience. This joking together is something that fills their bowls of importance.

An example of a ritual that emptied a little girl's bowl of importance was her dad's need to be at every one of her brother's football games. This hurt because her dad had only attended one of her dance recitals over the past three years. She was telling me she felt unimportant. You need to show up for the special occasions of each child's life. If you cannot show up, arrange to have the performance, either sports or art, filmed. Then sit down with your child and watch it together.

Finally, listen to yourself; don't give yourself an excuse to bow out of activities that are important to your child. If they skateboard, study skateboarding. I am not saying you need to make it your activity. Learn enough about it so you can have an intelligent conversation with your child. Spend the time to find out what he likes about skateboarding. Don't presume you already know as much as your child. Let him take you into his world.

Every family can make its own rituals of importance. They may be elaborate, like tea parties, or simple like turning all telephones, televisions, etc., off during family mealtime. In that way, you state "my family is more important than all those interruptions."

On the other side of the coin are rituals that teach children they are not the center of the universe. This is less critical early in life, but as they get older, they need to understand that others are important too. Family chores or volunteer activities are key rituals that can serve this function. Such rituals and the need for them will be covered more in depth in the next chapter on respect.

What channel markers let me know I'm still in the channel?

Importance is created when your children learn they are special to you and other members of their family. However, in teaching them to believe they are special, they need to know they are no more or less special than their siblings. The point is to divert them from the paths of believing they are so special that other people must wait on them or they are so insignificant that they are unimportant to all around them.

In each chapter, I have cited markers that let us as parents know our parenting boat is headed for the shoals—that we are no longer in the channels. Some, like the last one (i.e., "Good things come to those who wait") are old wisdom. Others have been picked up along the way. The following is a "Denzelism." Denzel Washington, director of the movie *The Great Debaters*, had a father character say the following to his son in the movie.

- ***Importance Channel Marker #1: "Do what you gotta do so you can do what you wanna do."***

Part of what helps us stay in the channel of true importance is teaching our child true esteem. Children know when adults are using fake praise. A child builds her true esteem when granted a compliment that has basis in solid reality. Saying to a child, "I love your drawing," is different than saying, "I love your choice of color," or "You draw people really well." Compliments that are concrete go into children's true esteem. They have earned them.

Children can sometimes look arrogant by believing they are the best at everything. It is important for them to know they may be the best runner in their class. However, as they grow, that might change because the others will be practicing. If being good at running is important to them and they have a natural talent, they must develop that talent with practice. Children will tell me they don't need a class 'cause they already know how. I let them know they may know as much as any nine-year-old, but to be as good at drawing as a sixteen-year-old, they will need an art class.

Other children become afraid and discouraged. When they are no longer special through talent alone, they give up. They don't feel brave enough or encouraged enough for the effort to continue to pursue their goal. I often use my Michael Jordan story.

When a child comes in and tells me he's the best at basketball or other things, I tell them I grew up in the land of North Carolina, the land of basketball. That's where Michael Jordan grew up. Do you know him? He is Mr. Basketball, the best basketball player ever.

Did you know he did not make the A squad the first year of high school? He made the B squad and went home and practiced and practiced. In fact, he practiced more than anybody else all through high school, college, and his professional career. He was talented, but his practice made him extraordinary.

Why do I do this? Because I want the child to understand what is necessary to become special and important in the bigger world outside his family.

Getting Back in the Channel:

When a child seems to be acting arrogant, it's important for her to learn what more will be expected of her as she grows. Gather some biographies of people that give her perspective.

When your child is discouraged and does not believe in herself and her possibilities, show her people who have succeeded through hard work and courage. Some of these biographies should be of people who succeeded when doctors or teachers had told them they never would. Your local librarian or bookstore salesperson can help guide you to age appropriate books on this topic for your child.

- ***Importance Channel Marker #2: Don't let an IT interfere with an US.***
Part of the growing process for children is to develop an understanding that others, parents and other people, are important too. I first identified this marker when problems arose between parents and their children over televisions and computers. There are an ever-increasing number of fights between parents and their children about Game Boy, Nintendo, Wii, and other computer games. Once the child begins, he seems unable to stop. He pleads with his parents that he will lose all his gains if he has to suddenly disconnect. According to the child, he has to reach a certain point. Then of course he scores a new win and cannot stop at that point either. Mothers and fathers nag and complain. They can't get their child to come to the dinner table or to start getting ready for bed. Their child won't turn off the computer long enough to talk about turning off the computer.

"ITs" are things like computer games, computers, and television in the parent-child relationship. "ITs" take away from the sense of working together as a team, as a family. They take away from loving relationships. When an *IT* becomes more important than an *US*, a precedent is set for a disconnect. For in that moment, the person is no longer present for the relationship. It is important to remember love is making a commitment to be with another.

If the issue for a child is entertainment, the lesson becomes one of decentering, in other words, learning to take into account another person's perspective. How do you, as a parent, help the child learn his impact upon you and the rest of the family by his total self-absorption in an act of entertainment? A boundary needs to be set to help the child learn to balance the needs of others versus self. To be so self-absorbed is not going to aid the child as a social being growing up and living in the community. Learning to balance the needs of self and other is an ongoing process that needs to be carefully nurtured in our families.

When the child does not learn boundaries around computers, etc., his social skills "muscles," which are already weak, become weaker. If the parents do not set limits in this area, the child doesn't have the time to practice other skills (e.g., when Sean plays computer games four hours per day, he has four less hours to interact socially with his friends and family). All children need time to practice their cognitive, social, and emotional skills of being human.

> **Sean's Game Boy**
> Recently, Sean came into my office playing his Game Boy. He had played it in the car ride from school to my office and while waiting for his appointment. He continued to play as he walked into my office. He continued to manipulate the game as we were talking. Sean and I have known each other a long time. Sean knows there are many games and other things to play with in my office. We play as we talk. However, the play we do is interactional: we play basketball, soccer, hockey, draw, create with the clay, and do sand work together. There is no way to join in a one-person handheld computer game. I could allow him to teach me about the game, but that would be the limit of the interaction. I explained to Sean that playing the game defeated the purpose of his time with me, that I was there for him for that hour.

Sean has social problems. Often, he ignores or disregards other people. When he is not doing this, he frequently misinterprets what other people are saying to him. He comes to me to learn social skills. He needs practice. His mom says he will have a friend over and not know how to be with him. When the friend tires of the computer, Sean refuses to stop. He refuses to try any other activities with his guest. Sean now has few friends. Sean has to learn to stay present by not disappearing into a machine. If he stays present, he could learn that his refusal to do anything his guests would like to do upsets them. He can learn to hear what they have to say and build friendships. This requires balancing the needs of self against the needs of his friends.

Getting Back in the Channel:

The way out of the problem is to understand that the *IT* is interfering with the *US*. Often, that involves one part of the *US* pointing out that there have now been three, four, five...times where the *IT* has become an argument that caused hard feelings between the *US*. Once that is explained, then a balance can be struck, which honors the desire (rather than the need) for one partner to have *IT* and the needs of the *US*, which are represented by the other partner. Clearly, boundary lines need to be delineated. Sometimes it helps the *US* if the other part of the dyad joins in with the *IT* on some occasions. In parent-child relationships, the parent can learn the computer game and play it with her child.

It always amazes me when I explain this marker to children. They get it right away. Of course they love their mommy better than their computer game. Often they even tell me that Mommy should hide their game. It is so clear to them people are more important than things. I hope, with this marker, such clarity and simplicity will be seen by all.

- ### Importance Channel Marker #3: Don't overlook a gift of love.

There is no one right way to give love. There are many. Love comes in the investment of time, in the risk of honesty, and in the ability to set limits. Love is demonstrated by the energy of the relationship. Love is not necessarily in the cost or materialism of the gift. Many people are confused by this today. They feel loved if they are given a large or expensive gift. Yet many people I know who receive or give these kinds of gifts realize that there may be many reasons behind such a gift other than love. People who give expensive gifts may be feeling guilty or ashamed. They may be trying to purchase your love or loyalty. There can be many motivations other than love.

Love is a daily gift. It comes in the form of giving your time to help someone solve a problem, to cook them a cake or dinner, to make them a gift or card, to listen to your loved ones' joys or problems. Love is exchanged in each interaction when we stop our busy agenda and become present to the person we love. That presence brings with it a gift of caring, a gift of honoring.

Parents give their children love when they read a book to them. They set aside their own needs when they read the same book for the hundredth time. A parent gives love when they perform a long set of routines every night that signal to a child that it is bedtime. A parent tells his child she is important when he lets go of his own boredom with the same routine night after night and provides the routine yet again to help her be secure and therefore be able to fall asleep. Each time, it is an act of love. Such a routine is also an act of love through limit setting. It seems far easier at the moment not to perform the ritual and be erratic in the bedtime routine. In the short run, it may be easier not to deal with the arguments of "I'm not tired," and let the child stay up. However, in recognizing their child's need to get enough sleep, in recognizing the child's inability to judge the consequences of the lack of sleep on themselves and their families, the parents, out of love, hold to a structure they believe is best for their child.

Children return love with a smile. Child learn as they grow that love is a mutual act. They learn that they feel love by giving love. They give love when they stir the cookie batter, set the table, or unload the dishwasher. When they give love, they feel important. They feel as if they have contributed to the family. This form of contribution helps them feel as if they belong in the family. Children can be taught that they are not simply recipients of love, but are great givers in everyday acts and on special occasions.

My daughters each have special dishes they prepare on family holidays. In the early days, I was by their side doing most of the work, but making sure they each did simple tasks in each dish's preparation. Now I do nothing except buy the ingredients at the grocery store. Members of the family each contribute to holiday meals. My daughters are proud of their contributions each year.

At Christmas, in my household, my daughters from three years of age on have handmade gifts for those people with whom we exchange gifts. Every year, we take time out to discuss what they are giving this year. When they were little, it might have been a drawing or a hand-painted card. As they grew, they made ornaments, candles, or soaps. The idea was not the cost, but the love and energy behind the gift.

The following stories provide two sides of the importance channel.

> **Lucas Wants Attention**
>
> Lucas is in the fourth grade. His mom and dad are very busy professionals. Lucas really wants his father's attention. Dad leaves for work before Lucas rises to go to school and frequently works until seven or eight o'clock. Lucas wins an honor in the science fair at school one day. He is very excited and wants to tell his father about it. His Dad has not even seen the project. Lucas stays awake until his dad comes home. When his dad comes home, he goes straight to his computer to continue his work.
>
> Lucas goes up to his dad and says, "Dad!" five or six times to try to get his attention. Dad does not acknowledge Lucas is even there. Finally, Mom comes up behind Lucas and says, "Peter, your son is trying to talk to you." Peter finally stops long enough to let Lucas show him his award. Unfortunately, this is a common situation.

Obviously, Dad is addicted to work and has little time for anything else, even his own son. Lucas is trying to let his dad know that he loves him; he wants some expression of love back. At some point, Lucas may realize that doing well in school does not get his father's attention. Maybe he will try doing something much less constructive in the future to see if that works.

> **Trixie's Demands**
> Trixie is fourteen and a handful. Her parents are worried about her. They worry she never seems to get enough. For instance, this weekend, she wants to meet her friends and roller-skate. This will require Mom to pick up three friends; the others will meet them at the rink. Mom agrees and says it will work best for her and Dad if they skate from 4:00 to 7:00 PM. Trixie pushes Mom, asking if they can skate from 3:00 to 8:00 PM, then finally blows up saying, "You never do anything for me."
>
> Mom, upset, says, "Trixie doesn't count what we can do. It makes me believe she will never be happy."

Children with Trixie's attitude have often been given too much attention and have a feeling of too much self-importance. They do not have any more self-esteem than those in Lucas's situation; they just expect more from others.

Getting Back in the Channel:

We all need to try to be aware of the little things our loved ones do for us. Sit back occasionally and think about the past week. *What special favors or expressions of love did I receive? How can I return these gifts of love? Am I more important than others? Can I begin the change needed to say I am important but they are too?* This is where the process of teaching a balance of self- and other-importance also teaches the beginnings of mutual respect.

A gift of love can come in many forms, like opening the manual garage door for your daughter or leaving an upbeat note in a child's lunchbox. What all gifts of love have in common is that they recognize a connection to the other and in some way express concern and care for them. Notice them, collect them—we need all that are given. By taking in these gifts of love, we recognize to whom we are important.

Conclusion

How do I help my child feel important? As your child grows, so will your expectation that she can tolerate frustration while you answer her sister. As your child grows, you will give her privileges that are consistent with her age. With those privileges will come responsibilities. She will learn to balance her own needs with others' needs.

Important does not mean getting waited upon by others. If your child has a special dance recital, it may mean she needs more help in getting ready and getting there. However, she will need to learn she needs to help when her brother has a soccer tournament. Balance is the key.

Importance means what is important to me is also important to my parents. Parents must exercise their ability to "sit in the shoes" of their child. Sometimes parents may wish to belittle something that is very important to their child. Fighting about who sits in a certain seat, who opens the Advent calendar, etc., may seem unimportant to parents. A child is important and gets balance when a parent accepts his need to be upset and does not let his upsetness destroy the family gathering. A child is important when he is asked to help provide a solution to the issue about which he is upset.

CHAPTER FIVE
How Do I Help My Child Gain Respect?

As the child grows and incorporates the teachings of the world, whether she is working at school, music, athletics, or the responsibilities of daily life, she learns that she *can* succeed, that she *can* complete what she starts. During the elementary school years, a child attempts to learn at school, to be industrious. She gains skill by doing her work and doing things. She makes things both with her parents and her peers. As a school-age child, she gains a sense of respect and a sense she can do enough. This is called industry.

If, for some reason, we expect too little of our child or disrespect her, she feels she *can't* succeed, not that we have made a mistake in our assessment of her. This sense of "can't" or inferiority is disabling. She will not try, often becoming depressed. The sense of *can* is built within the home by participating in family chores as well as at school and with her hobbies or sports.

On the other side of industry is the child who tries too hard, overfunctions, and does not get that the problem of not enough resides in us as parents not in him. The child feels this disrespect and fears he cannot do enough. Again, we need to balance the industry, the sense of "I can do" versus the inferiority, the sense of "I can't; I am incapable." The balance needs to be toward industry but being respectful of self and other. Respect is gained first from others trusting us, helping us to meet our own goals. It is sustained as we learn to respect ourselves. This respect of self shows in the demands we make of ourselves and clearly demonstrates to others that we are worthy of respect.

What is respect?

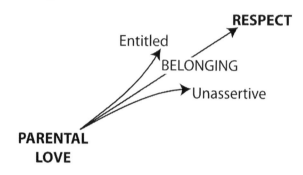

The *Oxford English Dictionary* defines respect as, "to treat or regard with esteem, deference or honor." Respect of self and other are integrally connected. All children deserve to be treated honorably and respectfully. However, as they grow, they need to learn that respect is mutual.

All children want to belong. They want to belong to their families, their friendship circles, and finally their world of school or work. Parents eventually cannot help their child belong outside the family. In fact, what parents can do is help their child learn what he has to do in order to belong. Belonging is not a given outside the family unit. Belonging is earned by participation in the work of life. This work may be schoolwork or it may simply mean acknowledging a friend's gift of time by playing with him. Parents can help a child learn what gifts he is given, what his responsibilities are to those gifts, and what his responsibilities are to himself.

The stories below present one child, Kai, who struggles on the entitlement side of the channel; another, Deena, who is sailing through the middle of the respect channel; and one, Dylan, who struggles on the other side of the channel with unassertiveness.

Kai's Story: A Story of Entitlement

Kai is back at college at twenty-one. He had gone the first semester after high school and had dropped out after not attending many of his classes or doing his work. He said the teachers were bad. Kai does have a learning disability and spent the last years of high school in a special education program. He now has decided to quit his job with which he has been successful and try college again. He starts back at a local community college.

Kai approaches his parents and states they owe him college. They did help his sister with her bachelor's degree, which she finished in four years with good grades. Kai states clearly they need to pay his apartment rent and his tuition. His parents had told him when he had dropped out before, he would have to pay for his own tuition and they would reimburse him if he had a C or better in the class. The parents feel guilty and renege on their statement from two years ago.

Kai quits his job, gets school loans, and proceeds to spend the money on concerts and technology. He believes his parents should pay for his rent and tuition. The parents don't like conflict and give Kai the money he believes he is owed. In the middle of the semester, Kai has car trouble. He tells his parents they need to buy him a new car. All the while, Kai is struggling at school. He has to drop a class and needs a tutor to help him pass math.

Kai believes the school is supposed to help him more because he has attention deficit disorder. He asks his mother to call the learning center to be sure he gets help.

> Kai talks to the school and decides next year he would like to transfer to the university. Kai wants to be a doctor, and the university is the best place for premed.

At no point does the school or the parents sit down with Kai to talk about the requirements for admission to the university. Kai, at this point, believes he will receive whatever he wants despite his own behavior. Wouldn't it be more respectful to point out that university admission requires a 3.5 or better GPA? Kai currently barely has a 2.0. Kai states that he can play the "D" card (disability) and exceptions will be made.

> **Deena's Story: A Story of Respect**
> Nineteen-year-old Deena wants to transfer from the large public university where she attended her first year of college. Her parents are aware she was very unhappy there her freshman year. However, the small private school she wishes to transfer to is the same school her boyfriend attends. Mom and Dad are adamant they will not let her go to that college as they believe she only likes it because her boyfriend is there. "That's no reason to choose a college," Mom says. Deena says she's done the research. The school has an excellent faculty in her major. She knows many of the other students at the school because of the times she's visited her boyfriend. She feels isolated at her large school and wants to be part of a smaller community. She realizes it could be hard if she and her boyfriend break up, but she really likes the school better.

Deena has done her research. She wants to author her life. Her parents are afraid for her. They are concerned that Deena chose the large school because she had friends going there. Now she's choosing the small school because of her boyfriend. This is a "both-and" situation in that her parents are probably right and Deena is an intelligent young lady who has done her research. To respect Deena, the parents decide they will support her decision. They do so with some reticence, fearing that if her boyfriend breaks up with her, she will be hurt. In the end, Deena's boyfriend did break up with her. However, Deena graduated from the liberal arts college, made good friends, and took away many good memories. This all occurred because her parents let go of their fear and allowed Deena to author her own life. Authorship means we can make mistakes and still know it was a good choice.

> **Dylan's Story: A Story of Unassertiveness**
>
> Dylan is a shy, introverted young man by nature. He works hard to get good grades. He is in tenth grade at a large urban high school. Dylan is sweet and considerate and, as a good firstborn, works hard to meet the expectations of both of his parents. His mother is a nurse and expects both of her children to do their work, get good grades, and excel at their extracurricular choices. Dylan is very perfectionistic and always feels he is disappointing himself and his mom and dad. This is despite the fact that he is an A-student, a great tennis player, and a good musician.
>
> Dylan sees on the grade portal for school that he has a D in science. There is an O for a paper he handed in three weeks ago. He remembers handing it to the teacher, but the grade is not there.

As we talk in session, it becomes clear he has not asked her about the paper. He has the paper still on his home computer. We talk about printing it out again and resubmitting it. This would be done with a note or discussion that he had handed it in on time originally. Dylan had a very difficult time accepting that teachers can make mistakes, and it could be all right to ask the question.

How does respect change over time?

The last channel the parent and child navigate is the channel of respect. At the beginning of the child's life, the parents take the responsibility to care for the child and the family. The needs of the infant and young child are great, and his capabilities are limited. This external source of caretaking by the parents supplies the sense of belonging. As the child grows, however, the child must assume some responsibilities within the family in order to gain that sense of belonging. Again, this process is not linear. Children develop and responsibilities develop with two steps forward and one or two steps backward. One day, he remembers his jobs; one day, he forgets. Eventually, in adulthood, he must assume the responsibility to care for himself without the need for external help and, in doing so, feel like he belongs in the larger world.

Respect

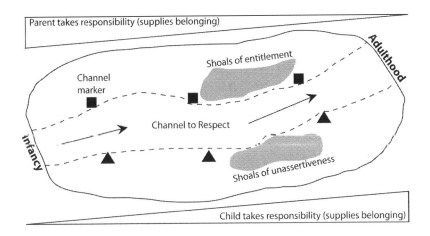

If the child is overindulged and waited on hand and foot, he will likely end up on the shoals of entitlement. Parents sometimes mistake overindulging for respect. The child will not learn the responsibilities required to maintain a relationship to which he wants to belong if this occurs. He will be resentful when anything is asked of him, feeling like he is entitled to the same treatment with which he grew up. On the other hand, some parents expect and demand the child take on challenging responsibilities far beyond his developmental capabilities. Such a child may grow into the position thrust upon him and may outwardly appear to be a competent, assertive individual. However, such a child, and adult, is very unassertive when it comes to his own needs. On this shoal of unassertiveness, he will place the needs of others above his own. The result of overfunctioning and subsequent invisibility can lead eventually to depression.

Can respect be lost and regained?

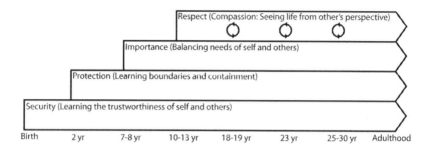

Respect, when it is taught to young children, is much more like limits or boundaries that help your child begin to feel as if she belongs. However, as the brain grows, so does the ability to have compassion. The ability to consistently show compassion may not be completely established until the child is in her twenties.

Many children demonstrate compassion for another child or person when they are not part of a problem. Children raised money for the children in Haiti after the hurricane. That is the beginning. Whether there is a child in Haiti or a child on the playground who is hurt, this demonstrates the beginnings of compassion or empathy. The most difficult form of compassion is to see the other person's perspective when we are part of the problem. The ability to see this type of problem from another person's perspective takes much longer to develop. Unfortunately, there are many adults who have never gained this ability.

If parents have not developed the ability to demonstrate compassion for the other in a relationship, it will not be a skill they can teach their child. In this case, it is incumbent upon those of us in the rest of the community around the child to demonstrate and encourage mutual respect.

Notice that I begin the notion of respect between ten and thirteen years of age. At that point, the child is further into the world and you will no longer be there to protect him at all times. It is also at this age that children often first encounter bullying at school, on the bus, etc. Bullying by definition is disrespectful. As we say in my office, "It's not cool to be cruel." At this age, the child may or may not want to talk to you about the experience, feeling he should handle it.

A child who has grown up in a household with respect may be confused by the behavior of such a peer. One little girl, who was very hurt by her bully, once said to me, "They must have a really bad mommy and daddy to act that way." This is not necessarily true. Bullies may have learned bullying from a sibling, or they may have been bullied by someone outside their family. One element is true. There is a perpetrator somewhere. Agel, in his book *The Radical Therapist*, developed the rescue triangle between a victim, a perpetrator, and a rescuer. We want our children to learn to stay away from all three roles.

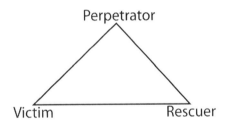

Where there is one role, there will be all three. In fact, the victim one day will be seen as a perpetrator and the rescuer the next day. Perpetrators only think of asserting/projecting self and self-respect. Victims are consumed with the needs (not having enough) of self and self-respect; whereas rescuers think of respecting others to the detriment of self-respect. Remember, respect is a balance of self- and other-respect.

We begin to establish this balance during our middle school and junior high years, and we rebalance it during later points in our lives. We learn how to belong when we start college. When we create a long-term relationship with another, such as marriage, we have to determine how to have respect for both ourselves and our partner. Yet another shift occurs as we begin parenting. As with all goals, respect is lost and regained. However, once gained, like liquid in a bowl, you can add to it or take away from it, but it would have to be a very big trauma to empty it completely.

What are some rituals that can help my child feel respected?

Respect is mutual. We teach our children to feel respected by first teaching them to give respect. When children are little, respect is taught by teaching manners.

In my office, children often choose to play the game "Mind Your Manners." It fascinates me that the children who choose the game most often come from chaotic, random families—the families who have weak structures and boundaries. The children seem to be looking for the rules of social interaction. In the game, you move forward toward winning when you get a positive card (e.g., waiting to go in the elevator until the people in it have left, listening to your teacher). You go backward when you play a negative card (e.g., chewing food with your mouth open, eating peas with your spoon, etc.). Many children are simply amazed at what might be considered by others as good or bad manners. They all are excited by the game, ask me questions, and are eager to learn.

A ritual of teaching good manners is a good place to begin the journey toward respect. This should be done with respect, not as punishment or something about which to fight. Saying "There's a secret you do not know" is a good way to begin to teach manners. Manners are customs and vary from culture to culture.

In Japan, people leave their shoes at the door of the home. Many children seem to know that. However, in the South where I grew up, children said, "Yes, sir," and "No, ma'am." They would address adults as Mr., Mrs., or Miss. If given permission today, they might use a first name, but until given permission, the title would be used as a form of respect. My children grew up knowing that in large family gatherings, they should ask permission to be excused from the table. Although that tradition was not necessary when our family ate alone, at Christmas gatherings, they would use their manners. We made a distinction between formal manners and manners within the home. For instance, it was okay to lick your bowl at home after eating a bowl of ice cream but not at other people's houses.

Along with the manners above, it was important to learn to greet someone who greeted you or to say, "Thank you," and "You're welcome." As a child with autism, Temple Grandin grew up in the 1950s and 1960s. She was coached by her mother in simple social skills. As a person with autism, these skills did not come naturally. Temple's mother held her accountable despite her disability, which later helped her function in the adult world of work.

A small way parents begin to say respect is mutual is by knocking on their children's bedroom doors before entering. This begins to establish what is expected of the child with regard to respect by demonstrating it. Respect is mutual.

Can you think of rituals your family has developed that teach respect?

Are there channel markers that let me know if I'm still in the channel?

The channel of importance is connected to the channel of respect. True respect of ourselves and of others is gained through acts that teach us about belonging. That is why not overlooking a gift of love teaches us importance. Recognizing that gift and giving back teaches us about belonging.

When we build belonging and mutual respect, we recognize what our child does that contributes to the family. We recognize and change those expectations as the child becomes more capable.

In so doing, we respect the growth of their abilities, their bodies, and their brains.

- **Respect Channel Marker #1: *Don't bite the hand that feeds you.***
This is an old adage. However, it is my experience that many people don't understand its basic premise. In all relationships, there is an exchange. In a parental relationship, mothers and fathers make an unspoken agreement to take care of their child. The child agrees to receive guidance and nurturing by growing.

In the parent-child relationship, there is always some interaction of both dependency and interdependency. Recognition of that dependency does not require subservience or feeling less than the person upon which you depend. However, it does help to recognize there is wisdom, knowledge, or a skill set that one person has that the other does not. That recognition does not mean that as the less knowledgeable one, the child has to live life the same way as the parent. It simply means the parent knows something about which the child is still learning. Sometimes difficulties arise in the parent-child relationship when the child wants to proceed in a different way than his parent. This needs to be a nonissue since there are many ways to solve a problem even if the child accepts what the parent is telling him about her knowledge. There are many ways to get to the same end.

However, a true problem exists when the child rejects the parent as not knowing, being stupid, or simply not worth the time to listen to. When someone is trying to help you in life, to reject him as worthless is biting the hand that feeds you; putting down or harming a helping person is not an option.

In parenting, we must teach our child about the nature of relationships. We must teach her to recognize someone's time or energy as a gift, to recognize that even if we disagree with the person who teaches us, we must always treat that person with respect. This is taught by helping children notice what they have and are receiving. It is taught by mutual respect. To accomplish these things, children must remain present to notice what is being given to them and to be grateful for all gifts.

> **Susie's Rudeness**
> Seven-year-old Susie came to the table for dinner. She immediately sat down and complained, "Oh yuck! Mom, I don't like tuna-fish casserole. Why did you fix this?"
> Mom, who had had a hard day at work sighed and thought, *Susie loved tuna-fish casserole last week.* Mom felt discouraged and angry.

There are many ways this could be handled. She could be told that tuna-fish casserole is her dinner and she has no other choice. She could be allowed to fix her own peanut-butter-and-jelly sandwich. There are many different parenting books to help a parent figure out the best solution for each family. However, I believe the issue goes beyond just how to handle dinner. It is important for Susie to learn she has a mutual responsibility. She depends upon Mom to fix her dinner. Mom loves her and willingly does so. Fixing dinner is a gift Mom gives her family. Susie needs to learn you don't emotionally slap people who have worked hard for you. She, in essence, slaps Mom when she complains. Don't bite the hand that feeds you.

Children are egocentric. They see things from their point of view. The process of parenting is to help children decenter as they grow—help them learn to be able to see things from another person's point of view. The lack of this ability in the adult world would be a handicap and lead to someone who could not form healthy relationships. The decentering process is nurtured when your eight-year-old asks you to get him a drink when he is standing closest to the refrigerator. By pointing out that he is capable and closest to the refrigerator, you teach him to see things from another's point of view. When your teenager points out that he is doing you a favor by driving the old car, rather than you buying him a better car like his friends drive, you can state, "Your driving the old car means the money that might have gone to a new car can be used to pay for our home." This statement asks him to see things from another perspective. It asks him to leave his egocentric stance.

In families, children get used to being a recipient. They need to be taught their responsibility at each juncture. Their responsibility at minimum is to act respectfully to their caregivers, be they parents, babysitters, teachers, or day-care workers. Respect is their side of the contract. They may not like the person, and they may disagree with the person, but they can respond with respect. Respect needs to be the basis of all relationships. The teacher may be unfair, may have favorites, may even need to be changed, but still needs to be respected in your response. The teacher's intention is to teach even if the student disagrees with how the subject is being taught.

The next level after respect is to provide the teacher, parent, etc., with some level of gratitude. Actually, the expression of gratitude varies with the relationship and the feelings. Even if you disagree with the parent or teacher, learning to acknowledge that this person is trying to teach or help, even though it doesn't feel that way, is important in the decentering process. It is important to remember that a thank-you is both for the person to whom you say it and for yourself. By acknowledging the other, you feel better about yourself.

Getting Back in the Channel:

The first step in getting back in the channel is for each family member to reexamine his or her own role. If one member overfunctions, that person should stop. He or she cannot make the others function but does have a choice about overfunctioning. You don't have to get milk for a child who is screaming at you, nor do you have to cook dinner for people who put you down. It is always interesting to see what happens if you just simply stop. If you are all adults, do the other adults pick up the slack? If you are fixing dinner and you stop, eventually everyone will get hungry and may help in order to get the meal on the table.

Part of being in a healthy relationship is not destroying the person with whom you relate. That destruction can be by working that person to death or simply by hurting the person who is consistently there for you. Don't bite the hand that feeds you.

The alternative side is expecting too much from the child and not listening to her; she then feels bitten. She becomes unassertive and will not ask for what she needs or wants. Neither shoal will work. Parent the boat toward mutual belonging and respect.

- **Respect Channel Marker #2: To feel love is to give love is to feel love.**

Children are full of love when they are born. As they grow and receive more love, they have more and more love to give. The way children give love is in the form of a smile, a coo, and, in the end, a settling in to the security and protection you provide them through consistency and limits. This could be in setting a consistent bedtime or redirecting aggressive energy. Many people think of the parent-child relationship as one-way. The parent gives; the child receives. However, it is through the impact the child has upon her environment that she learns about belonging. Whether you're four and you help Mom make cookies for the family by stirring the batter or you are a teen and you help your family by making a meal, when you give love by helping, you feel love.

In contrast, if you are not asked to help the family, you feel useless or unimportant. It may very well seem as if the family could do without you. I can think of nothing as painful as feeling incompetent or useless. Schools often unintentionally do a very good job of making our children feel incompetent. There are so many skills to learn, and they cannot all be our strengths. We come home to remember we belong. We do not learn about belonging by watching television or playing computer games. We learn about our belonging when we do something that is important to our families. As a result, we feel important. We believe ourselves to be important and competent family members.

> **Bjorn's Homework**
> Sixteen-year-old Bjorn plays football at school and is an A student. When he comes home, he crashes, watches television, and plays on the computer. His mother is a teacher; she works all day and then comes home to all the family tasks, such as dinner and laundry. Mom and Dad bring Bjorn into therapy because they are worried that Bjorn does not begin his homework until 9:00 PM. Mom is afraid he is risking his grades and that he needs to learn time management.

It becomes clear as we talk that Mom resents having no help from Bjorn with dinner or at home. She says she and Dad are constantly available to help him, but he does not seem to give back. Mom and Bjorn had to work to reframe the issue. Bjorn is not incompetent at school. He does have a time-management issue: he waits to start his homework until 9:00 PM and plays on his computer until that time. That is Bjorn's problem. Given his history as a student, Mom needs to let go of this time-management issue except when he expects help at 11:00 PM to edit a paper. She needs to state clearly she is not available to assist him after 10:00 PM and hold to that limit.

Finally, there is an issue between the two of them about him contributing to the family. They need to work out a plan of how and when he is expected to help with dinner. They need to set limits clearly stating when a job needs to be done (e.g., taking out the trash no later than 10:00 PM on Monday night). They need to agree and sign a contract about those responsibilities. They also need to agree what happens if Bjorn does not follow through (e.g., if he is on the computer and misses the trash or any other job, the computer room will be off limits for the remainder of the week except to work on a school paper).

> **Madelyn's Demands**
>
> Four-year-old Madelyn is the center of both her parents' and grandparents' universe. Grandmother notices that Madelyn is becoming more and more demanding as each adult seems almost in competition to make life fun for her. In fact, Madelyn recently reported that Grandma had been mean to her one day when she did not take her to Target on demand to buy a new toy. Grandma, being a wise woman, realized this was not Madelyn's fault, but the result of Madelyn needing to learn how to put other's needs ahead of her needs on occasion. Grandma asked her son and daughter-in-law if they could all help Madelyn learn.

The parents went to Madelyn and told her they had made a mistake in not helping her learn how important she was as a helper. From then on, when Madelyn spent time with Grandma, she knew she might need to be Grandma's helper. She would help Grandma straighten her jewelry tray or walk her dog. Madelyn began to see herself as an important helper and has quit talking about people being mean to her. She is also less demanding with her parents. She no longer views herself as a person to be entertained.

Getting Back in the Channel:

In a relationship, when only one person is giving and is not receiving love, the boat is straying out of the channel. Obviously, this is not true with infants and toddlers. But as the child develops, it is the job of the giving person to let the other know how he feels and what gifts of love he would like. Then, if necessary, the giving person needs to stop the giving. The parents should understand if they truly love their child, they must try to express it in ways that are calm and assured.

When one person underfunctions and another overfunctions in a relationship, the relationship becomes off balance. Your boat has too much weight distributed at one end, and it can sink. Part of helping children grow is helping them learn to give love as well as receive love. As a four-year-old, it might mean bringing your glass to the sink; as a seventeen-year-old, it might mean loading and unloading a dishwasher. The ability to give love and the forms that love takes grow as they grow. To feel love is to give love is to feel love.

- **Respect Channel Marker #3: You get what you get and don't throw a fit.**

This is a statement a kindergartner made in my office once. She said she had learned it from her kindergarten teacher. Simply stated, it means sometimes you don't get exactly what you wanted or dreamed, but you still can't throw a fit. It does not mean you can't express any wishes quietly to your parent or teacher. It does not mean you cannot have feelings and learn to ask your teacher if you can have your choice next time. It could be the purple tricycle. It could be the opportunity to be the teacher's helper if it's not clear how students take turns. It could mean having a different ice cream when you have already chosen and your friend's seems better.

If you don't throw a fit, in spite of your disappointment, you are learning self-discipline and practicing gratitude and respect for what you are given. Learning gratitude and respect for what you are given is the only avenue to feeling as if you are enough and have enough in life. Even though life is not all you dreamed, can it be enough?

> **Renuka's Story**
> Renuka is five years old and has a speech therapist who works with her at school. On the day I was observing her, she and another classmate were working on making their mothers a present for Mother's Day with their speech therapist. The therapist had brought two packages of animal graham crackers for a snack as they finished their session. She asked Renuka if she would like to choose her package. She chose. Then her classmate got her package. Renuka looked at the classmate and then the teacher. She said, "But I want that package."

Renuka is the youngest in her family and is used to complaining, whining, and sometimes screaming to get her way. Because her brother is significantly older and Mom hates conflict, her brother has learned just to give in.

On this day, the speech therapist calmly assured Renuka she would get to choose again the next time she met with her. Renuka quieted and simply ate her snack.

Getting Back in the Channel:

If you have a child who throws a fit when she does not have her way, do you give in? Do you escalate the battle by telling her she cannot have her way? It works better to state the fact: this is the way it is now, but you can choose next time. Simply state when her next opportunity will be to choose even though it may be a choice in a completely different part of the day or a choice on a different issue. The point is there are times she does get a choice. Tell her you're sure she can make a good choice then if she needs reassurance.

Remember: you get what you get and you don't throw a fit.

I hope these channel markers will help you navigate through your loving relationships. Safety is the basis of a loving relationship. By following the markers, all parties may be safe enough to endure the storms of life. The markers, as stated previously, are only meant to serve as stop signs or guides to what I have found works consistently. They, of course, are based on the assumption that you consider values, such as self- and other-respect, gratitude, reciprocity, responsibility, acceptance, presence, making amends, and boundaries to be important. There are many other markers along the channel. I do not pretend to know them all.

What interferes with my child feeling respected?

Many things can interfere with a child building a sense of mutual respect. In our society, many parents do too much for their children. When they are little, they need us to do much for them. However, as they grow, we need to let go of our doing. When my daughters were adolescents, their anger and disrespect was an important clue that I was doing too much for them.

Many things contribute to doing too much for your child. The fear of being judged a poor parent is a major contributor. Sometimes this fear causes parents to stray from their values. This is especially tragic when the value to be taught is respect—self-respect and other-respect. An example of this would be the fear of being judged by others as an unkind or unsupportive parent. Finally, some parents do too much because they are afraid if they don't, they will screw up their children, but actually, they are more likely to screw them up by doing too much. What would have happened if Mom hadn't run all those errands for Hannah who was away at college?

Parental overfunctioning occurs when a child is given the message that he is special, more special than anyone else. It is wonderful for a child to know he is loved and that you recognize and enjoy his uniqueness. However, you go too far when you teach him that others in the world think he is very special. That leads to a child who feels overly entitled.

When we give our children the message they are very special, this is a form of misplaced respect. Overly entitled children believe they do not need to follow the rules of society (e.g., complete homework at school). This sets them up for failure. No one outside the family will treat them that way. This is a recipe designed to produce children who feel overly entitled. They will not accept jobs they feel are beneath them. Ultimately, this will lead to an unhappy, unhealthy life.

In the book *50 Rules Kids Won't Learn in School*, author Charles Sykes talks about how feel-good, politically correct teachings created a generation of kids with no concept of reality. This concept sets them up for failure in the real world. In order to succeed in the adult world, Sykes says, kids need to learn the following rules:

- Rule 1: Life is not fair—get used to it!
- Rule 2: The world won't care about your self-esteem. The world will expect you to accomplish something BEFORE you feel good about yourself.
- Rule 3: You will NOT make $60,000 a year right out of high school. You won't be vice-president with a car phone until you earn both.
- Rule 4: If you think your teacher is tough, wait till you get a boss.
- Rule 5: Flipping burgers is not beneath your dignity. Your Grandparents had a different word for burger flipping—they called it opportunity.
- Rule 6: If you mess up, it's not your parents' fault, so don't whine about your mistakes, learn from them.
- Rule 7: Before you were born, your parents weren't as boring as they are now. They got that way from paying your bills, cleaning your clothes and listening to you talk about how cool you thought you were. So before you save the rain

forest from the parasites of your parents' generation, try delousing the closet in your own room.
- ➢ Rule 8: Your school may have done away with winners and losers, but life HAS NOT. In some schools they have abolished failing grades and they'll give you as MANY TIMES as you want to get the right answer. This doesn't bear the slightest resemblance to ANYTHING in real life.
- ➢ Rule 9: Life is not divided into semesters. You don't get summers off and very few employers are interested in helping you FIND YOURSELF. Do that on your own time.
- ➢ Rule 10: Television is NOT real life. In real life people actually have to leave the coffee shop and go to jobs.
- ➢ Rule 11: Be nice to nerds. Chances are you'll end up working for one.[2]

Sykes describes the real world. If we send our children out there with no preparation, we set them up for failure. If we continue to run their lives for them throughout college, when we do let go, where does that leave them? Wouldn't it be best if we let go more gradually and prepared them for the real world? If we don't gradually wean them from our help, but instead give them every advantage we can think of, we will increase the number of children who cannot succeed. Think back to your successes in life. Did you gain them while working through the bumps and bruises of the situation? Or were you handed the solution? An overfunctioning parent leads to an underfunctioning child. An over-responsible parent leads to an under-responsible child.

- **Fears that interfere with the development of respect**

What follows are two examples of how fears interfered with the development of respect within the child. In the Chang family,

---

2   Sykes, 50 Rules Kids Won't Learn in School: Real-World Antidotes to Feel-Good Education, p. 11-49.

neither parent stepped forward; neither wanted to play the "bad guy." They wanted Amy to learn by osmosis. There is a fear on the part of one parent of being disliked or the bad guy. In the Miller family, Dad is afraid his wife wants his son to be a wimp or a "rule follower." See how this sets up his son. By Mom and Dad not coming to an agreement about this, Dad actually role models disrespect of Mom and maybe female teachers.

- **Fear of setting limits**

    Fear is played out in all families. For many reasons (e.g., wanting to avoid conflict, being too busy, or not wanting to be disliked by the child), often only one parent is the limit setter. Parents learn eventually this simply won't work. Children misinterpret the passivity of the other parent. The parenting process lasts over so many years that the parent who has to play the "bad guy" will tire, wear out, and resent the other.

> **The Chang Parents**
>
> Mr. and Mrs. Chang are a middle-class family. Due to the economic shifts in his profession, Mr. Chang was unemployed the year before Amy started college. Amy was able to secure an excellent job through a connection with a friend. She earned twelve dollars per hour and worked forty hours per week. This job lasted twelve weeks. Mr. and Mrs. Chang sat Amy down at the beginning of the summer, and they all agreed she would need to save $2,500 over the summer to help pay for college because money was tight for the family. As the summer continued, Mr. and Mrs. Chang watched as Amy came home with more and more CDs. Amy was also eating out at restaurants with her friends. Although each was worried about Amy and her spending, no one said a word. Mr. Chang waited for Mrs. Chang. Mrs. Chang waited for Mr. Chang. At the end of the summer, Amy had a little over $300 in her savings.

Given that Amy had never had a job or a checking account, were all parties (Mom, Dad, and Amy) responsible? Amy clearly knew nothing about budgeting, saving, or following through with commitments. How could this have been handled differently? The Changs chose to make up for the amount Amy did not save, but what did Amy learn?

> **Miller Parents**
>
> Mrs. Miller came to me very concerned about her son, John, soon to be in ninth grade. She believed he was completely out of control. He used to be a straight-A student, but last year, his grades dropped until his only A was in physical education. Her son is the reason his school developed an honor code. He was selling his homework services to at least twenty of his peers before he was caught. She was concerned because he left on his bike for the day and came in when he pleased, and she didn't know where he was much of the time. Dad doesn't believe John needs to tell Mom where he's going. He is concerned, "She's trying to make him into a mama's boy." Dad clearly believes "boys need to be boys," and John doesn't really have any problems. He communicates this to his son, who now tells Mom, "I don't have to listen to you." John has run away two times this past year for two or three days. Rather than leave on a family vacation, he ran away, and the family left for a week after reporting him missing to the police. Dad is now thinking there might be a problem.

This is a complicated family. What would have been their son's course if Mom and Dad had sat down and agreed what they wanted their son to learn? Does Dad really believe his son will be feminized by respecting certain family rules? Does he believe men who cooperate within the family are less masculine? Or is this about Dad and Mom and a competition of who is to be the most important parent to their son? As for most important parent, Dad has clearly won since Mom is now functioning as a "persona non grata"—an invisible person to whom John doesn't even have to listen. The problem is that their son is not doing well in school or at home. Can they either identify or set aside their own needs in order to help John? No matter what the possible source for this acting out behavior, John is in constant trouble. Do they really want this trouble for John? Can they work toward a goal of creating a competent, caring, and contributing adult? They both have to sit and reassess how their choices are affecting their son.

- **Fear that the child will not have the "good life"**
In his poem on children, Kahlil Gibran explains that we do not live where our children live, for "their souls dwell in the house of tomorrow."

Of Children

And a woman who held a babe against
her bosom said, Speak to us of Children.
And he said:
Your children are not your children.
They are the sons and daughters of Life's
longing for itself.
They come through you but not from you,
And though they are with you yet they do
not belong to you.
You may give them your love but not your thoughts,
For they have their own thoughts.
You may house their bodies but not their souls,

> For their souls dwell in the house of tomorrow, which
> you cannot visit, not even in your dreams.
> You may strive to be like them, but seek not to make
> them like you.
> For life goes not backward nor tarries with yesterday.
> You are the bows from which your children as living
> arrows are sent forth.
> The archer sees the mark upon the path of the infinite, and
> He bends
> you with His might that His arrows may go swift and far.
> Let your bending in the archer's hand be for gladness;
> For even as He loves the arrow that flies, so He loves also
> the bow that is stable.[3]

Gibran knew that we cannot completely prepare our children for their "good life" because they will live in the future, which is beyond our sight. I remind parents that we cannot completely prepare our children for a future we can't predict. Instead, we respect them by giving them strength, belief in themselves, and problem-solving skills for the challenges of a future that we cannot fully anticipate. As parents, we need to strike a proper balance between challenging in areas where they are not yet fully developed and reinforcing their strengths and gifts.

Parents want their child to have at least as good a life as they have had, but most want more for their child. They often want their child to have more—more happiness, resources, education, or freedom. It is difficult if not impossible to discern what it will take for the child to attain more. Parents feel as if they have to prepare their child for every contingency. However, in parents' fear that they have omitted something, they actually communicate to the child that somehow the child is not enough. This fear is compounded when parents obsess over any weakness their child has.

---

[3] Gibran, *The Prophet*, p. 17-18.

> **Daniel's Future**
> Daniel is a straight-A student and valedictorian of his high school. Daniel is quite shy and is not socially at ease in his peer group. Because of his introversion, advocating for himself is difficult—like having a weak muscle. He is far from arrogant and believes his accomplishments are not unusual. He was given a full scholarship to attend a prestigious university. I have known Daniel for many years, and he has wonderful parents who love him very much. As Daniel is about to graduate from college, his mother becomes increasingly concerned that he will not advocate for himself well enough to get a job, in spite of his academic success at the university. She wants me to meet with him to help him with his résumé and talk to him about interviewing and looking for jobs.

What does this say to Daniel if she sets up this appointment without his knowledge? Can Daniel ever be good enough? While Daniel is a wonderful son, like all of us, he is not perfect. How does Daniel interpret Mom's fear? Is it the result of his inadequacy? Is it just Mom doing all she can do to help?

How can Mom communicate her respect for Daniel?

I encourage Mom to talk to Daniel and tell him how very proud she is of him, tell him she is proud of his accomplishments and the wonderful way he used his time at college. Instead of making the appointment for him, she could simply remind him I am here to help if he wants assistance in this next stage of life. She could let him know I have experience in helping people with their résumés and with interviewing. At this point, she needs to let it go. It is now up to Daniel, at twenty-two years of age, to decide if he wants or needs help. He won't learn the skill of recognizing his needs and acting on them if she does these things for him. The very skill she wants him to learn is one he can practice in this situation. He may decide he would rather work with the career office at his school. It is up to Daniel. When Daniel sees the respect he has clearly earned, he will feel more confident to face his future. Remember, the "good life" from the parents' perspective is not necessarily the "good life" from the child's perspective. The adult child goes into a future we, as parents, cannot clearly see.

- **Feeling sorry for the child**

I talked earlier in the chapter on protection that feeling sorry for your child is one of the most destructive things you can do. I have mentioned Temple Grandin. She is probably the most famous adult alive who has autism. Grandin created a design for cattle stockyards that allows cattle to be slaughtered in a humane way. She attended school, including college and graduate school, at a time when most autistic children were institutionalized. Her mother had respect for her ability to learn. She not only learned academic subjects but also social rules. Her mother did not feel sorry for her. She was constantly asked to do her best in spite of her disability. In respecting her abilities, her mother gave her the opportunity to have a meaningful life.

Today, too often in trying to respect our children's disabilities or differences, we fail to respect their abilities. We advocate for them to the point we do not hold them accountable. This is disrespectful. Like in any other part of parenting, we must find a balance. It is not okay to put obstacles in their way (i.e., when Grandin's self-soothing or calming device was not allowed by her college). However, we must not allow them to believe they can use the "D" card (disability) and be absolved of their responsibilities in the adult work (i.e., the story of Kai).

Children in my office hear there are no passes. Each child struggles in one way or another. One child stated, "I have the A thing.

That means I can't do my homework" ("A" thing meaning attention deficit). I immediately reframe the "A" thing. "Oh that just means it is harder for you to do your homework. You still have to do it."

- **Having no ability to teach respect of others**

    Finally, we must deal with the parent who, for whatever reason (e.g., mental illness, childhood trauma, drug or alcohol addiction, etc.), does not have the ability to respect his children. The biggest problem with this is that it is confusing for the children. Sometimes the parent seems respectful. Sometimes the parent seems to be acting as if the child is important (e.g., Mom showing up at her performance). However, the inconsistent behavior makes it difficult for the child to determine why sometimes Mom shows up and not other times. To a child, it must be something she did wrong or maybe she is inherently bad, not worthy of respect from her parent.

    Often it has little to do with the child's needs. Sometimes parents use alcohol/drugs/work; sometimes they don't. Sometimes a parent uses in a way that makes a child believe it is not all right to be the center of attention. The center of attention must always be the parent. Other times, the child is only given importance or respect if Mom or Dad can bask in the glory the child is receiving. Even the glory becomes more about the parent than about the child.

    In no way am I saying this is intentional on the part of any parent I know. All the parents I have met love their children. However, because of some parents' excessive needs, the child does not have her own needs met. The parents' needs are just too deep for them to consistently be able to be there for their child.

Conclusion

How do I help my child gain respect? How can I help my child so she is not left to face all the struggles of a complex world alone? How can I help her to realize this is her life and she must author it, enjoying both the fruits and hardships on her own? Where are the limits? Where are the lines? Limits are difficult in a society that seems limitless. We seem to have unending choices. Rules by their very nature need to be questioned, but now we seem to have no rules. Without limits, there can never be enough. Enough is encountered when we reach that limit, that line. Many parents are uncertain where those limits are. They are hesitant to make a decision and stick with it. They cannot find a balance between being an authoritarian parent and a permissive parent. They struggle between "Do it because I say so and I am the parent" and "Whatever." Permissive parents teach their children to ignore rules, to disrespect others. Permissive parents inadvertently teach their children how to talk their way out of things. There are situations in which these traits will be an advantage; others in which they will not. Have you helped your child learn those differences?

When you do everything for your child, your skills in problem solving and life increase. In the process, your child fails to develop the skills he needs in order to grow.

So how do parents' fears of not doing enough affect their child's sense of respect? By overdoing for your child, you become more competent as your child becomes less competent. When you fail to teach your child how to fit in with others, your child acts entitled, demanding, and disrespectful. These traits will not lead to a happy childhood or happy adulthood.

When you do too little for your child, your child quits asking and becomes unassertive. She feels unworthy of your time and your attention. She feels abandoned, left alone to handle the world without the wisdom of an adult. This may result in a timid adult or an extremely competent, overachieving, overfunctioning adult. Both types of children carry a hole in their heart that you as the parent never filled.

Neither option is the way to help your child become a caring, competent, and contributing adult. Parents must strive for the middle ground. This permits their children to achieve their own successes while knowing they are loved for who they are and respected for their own interests and accomplishments. Parenting is the most difficult job you will ever do. There are many times you will want to help and must not. When you, as a parent, demonstrate compassion to your child without rescuing him you show him the way down the channel of respect.

CHAPTER SIX
How Do I Use This Information to Reach My Goal?

Parents often parent the way they were parented or do the opposite in reaction to the way they were parented. What I am suggesting is to think about your goals as a parent. The goal, as stated throughout this book, is to raise a competent, caring, and contributing adult. The goal is that at the end of the journey, the child who became the adult knows she is loved. As a parent, I will not have done everything right, nor do I expect she will do everything right. I want her to *trust* that she is competent to pursue what is best for her and yet she understands the *limits* to her pursuits. I want her to *belong* to a family, a set of friends, and/or the world so in case something happens to me, she will be surrounded by care. To receive caring, she must know how to care for others as well as herself. I want her to feel her life has meaning. She has the self-*esteem* to feel she is important. Importance is felt when she contributes to the world, not just takes from it.

The goals of parenting are intimately tied to the four channels of the parenting model. A child's trust in parents leads to trust in self, which in turn leads to security and a willingness to pursue his dreams. A child's sense of limits set by the parents leads to a realistic view of the world's limits and a balanced sense of protection, which provides emotional competency. A child's feeling of esteem provided initially by the parents is eventually replaced by esteem that comes from actual accomplishments, which in turn leads to a sense of importance and therefore confidence. Finally, by expecting the child to contribute to the family, parents engender in him a sense of belonging, which he then internalizes. The self-respect thus attained along with security, protection, and importance enables him to care for others and contribute to the world.

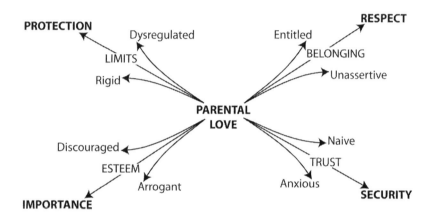

As I stated initially, there are many parenting books that address specific tasks of parenting (e.g., how to toilet train your child, how to handle a misbehaving child, etc.). This book is meant to be an umbrella: an umbrella that covers all children over their entire life cycle. I recognize that children are born different. Each child has his own strengths and challenges. However it is my fervent belief that it is incumbent upon us as parents to help our children get ready to enter the adult world and be able to function without us. Each of these strengths and limits must be addressed individually. You as a parent may need to read more about specific issues such as temperament, Asperger's syndrome, anxiety disorders, attention-deficit disorder, etc. However, as you journey down those roads, keep in mind your big picture: what do you want at the end? If your goals are similar to mine, this umbrella can help guide you down the safest channels.

HOW DO I USE THIS INFORMATION TO REACH MY GOAL?

Many parents get lost in responding to immediate needs. They are lost in the moment doing what they think will make the child happy, avoiding conflict, getting accommodations for their child from the schools so the child can pass, etc. This is by no means a bad thing. However, it is our role to think about where our parenting boat is headed. We need to think beyond the present moment to the skills our children need for their future. Are we too far out of the channel to help our child become a competent, caring, contributing adult? How do we gently and over time steer the boat back within the channel?

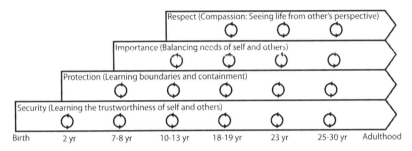

The life cycle model above shows each of the channels along with symbols indicating the cycling that occurs over a child's life. This diagram makes it apparent that each channel starts at different times but that as the child gets older, each previous channel gets revisited as both the parents and the child reach the necessary balance. The complexity of parenting may be daunting, but as long as we realize where we have been, we can know better where we need to go. We can intuitively understand that an infant needs to feel secure, that a two-year-old needs to be protected from the world and her own impetuousness, that a grade-school student needs to understand where she fits into a world that is wider than just her family, and that a junior-high student needs to understand how her feelings fit with what others are feeling. When we discover our parenting boat has strayed too close to the shoals, we need to be cognizant of these age-related factors if we are to return to the right course.

In the following examples, I will address how the models I have outlined can be used to see the next step needed in parenting to help your child get back into the channel.

What questions do I need to ask?

There are seven questions that you must answer in order to see the course to steer your boat:
1. What is the problem?
2. How old is the child?
3. What is happening in the child's world?
4. What channel(s) needs addressing?
5. How do I, as a parent, contribute to this problem?
6. What can I do differently?
7. If I have done the above, what do I need to learn more about that may be grounding my parenting boat?

Let's see how these seven questions work.

> ### Ellie at Four
> Mom and Dad are scared and seeking answers. Their cherished four-year-old girl, Ellie, is out of control. They seem to be screaming at her constantly and she, at them. She won't go to bed. She runs around the table instead of sitting and eating. Getting her dressed in the morning is a nightmare.

Mom and Dad wonder, *What will she be like at thirteen if she's like this at four? Are we complete failures as parents?*

I assure them that the truth is they have been loving parents, but they haven't provided their daughter with the structure and routine that she needs in order to feel secure or the limits that would offer her protection from her own willfulness. Since she

HOW DO I USE THIS INFORMATION TO REACH MY GOAL?

behaves well at preschool, there is no reason why she can't behave better at home.

As I speak with them, it becomes clear that neither parent has learned how to set limits with their daughter in a positive way. They approach their daughter by asking for her cooperation. After a while, if they don't get it, they become frustrated and start yelling. Although they are remorseful, they fail to recognize their fear of Ellie not liking them. They want her to like them as they ask her to cooperate. This lack of recognition that children often don't like to cooperate interferes with their ability to create a secure and protected family life for Ellie. While their daughter may not like these limits and structures, they are essential for her development.

- What is the problem?
  Ellie is out of control, yelling and not listening.

- How old is the child?
  Four years old

- What is happening in the child's world?
  Mom and Dad are not protecting Ellie from herself or her anger. They are not emotionally regulating and protecting Ellie from their yelling. Ellie seems to not know limits. Ellie has no routine or structure. She does not know the days of the week. She does not comprehend that some mornings are play mornings and some she must get ready to go to school. She does not understand the order of the day.

- What channels need addressing?
  Protection and security

- How do I, as a parent, contribute to this problem?
  Mom and Dad both want Ellie to like them. They start the day by implying she has a choice when she doesn't. When she

doesn't comply, they yell and scream and try to overpower her. Ellie believes people who yell and scream win. Mom and Dad, either due to ignorance or not taking the time, have not set a routine for Ellie and have not been consistent.

- What can I do differently?

  Mom and Dad can take the time to set up and agree upon a routine. They can draw pictures or cut out pictures that demonstrate the order of the routine. Then they can post this in Ellie's room or on the refrigerator.

  Mom and Dad can then discuss the routine with Ellie. When Ellie gets up, they can all defer to the chart on the refrigerator. They can laugh and see how quickly they can finish the steps.

  Mom and Dad need to be trustworthy. They need to be consistent. It is very easy to let routines slip. Ellie may then think the steps are optional, that she has the power to determine structure. Structure is determined by what we have to do that day. It is not whimsical and up for grabs each day.

  Mom and Dad need to think about how their fear of Ellie disliking something they do or their fear of Ellie's unhappiness is interfering with their need to teach Ellie. They may also need to think about how taking the time to set up a structure and providing routine saves a great deal of time later. We can use our time getting ready each morning letting the routine lead the way. Or we can use all our time each day yelling about whether the routine is necessary. It is more secure for Ellie if her parents just take it for granted and follow through with the routine.

- If I have done the above, what do I need to learn more about that may be grounding my parenting boat?

  Do research into temperament, attention deficit disorder, sensory defensiveness, and overindulgence.

HOW DO I USE THIS INFORMATION TO REACH MY GOAL?

> **Kalid Is Overwhelmed**
> Kalid has known me since he was six years old. I am simply referred to at school as the "worry doctor." Kalid is now eight, almost nine years old and in third grade. Summer is approaching. Kalid comes into my office and states clearly while we play basketball, "You have to help me with my parents."
> As I explore what is bothering Kalid, he talks about the fact that Mom is going to sign him up for eleven different weekly day camps over the summer. Both Mom and Dad are professionals with demanding careers and will only get two weeks off over the summer. Kalid says he is going to be signed up for a LEGO camp, a computer camp, a soccer camp, and the list goes on and on. Each week, there will be different children and different teachers. When Kalid was little, he had a nanny and they mostly stayed home and played. Kalid expresses his desire to have fewer changes and get to stay home more. He is overwhelmed by the changes summer will bring.

Mom and Dad come into the office the next week, and we talk about Kalid's need for consistency and routine. They want Kalid to develop some of his skills in certain areas. They recognize that he is overwhelmed by the number of changes that will be demanded of him in eleven different programs. Mom and Dad begin to see summer from Kalid's perspective.

To allow Kalid downtime, Mom and Dad do research and find a favorite babysitter of his who is available to stay with him at home during certain weeks. Mom and Dad decide to alternate one week each of their vacation staying at home with Kalid. That way, they will still have one week for a family vacation. With that juggling, they then went to Kalid to find out which of the types of day camp experiences interested him most. This reduced eleven changes down to five. Kalid thought he could handle those changes.

- What is the problem?

  Kalid is overwhelmed by the prospect of attending eleven different weekly day camps over the summer. At each camp, there will be new children, new teachers, and different rules.

- How old is the child?

  He is almost nine and will start fourth grade in the fall.

- What is happening in the child's world?

  Kalid has always had a nanny. At the beginning of third grade, Mom and Dad let the nanny go and started using before and after care at Kalid's school. This summer, because Mom and Dad both have demanding careers, they have chosen eleven different summer day camps. They believe these are all on topics Kalid will enjoy or needs to learn.

- What channels need addressing?

  Kalid is feeling unimportant since his parents are not listening to him. He also feels unprotected by his parents, which is causing him to be overwhelmed, a form of internal dysregulation. He would have eventually blown up, changing over to external dysregulation. Kalid is overwhelmed; his concerns need to be listened to and addressed. He is asking his parents to understand how many changes he can tolerate over the summer. What are the limits? Can his parents protect him?

- How do I, as a parent, contribute to this problem?

  Mom and Dad are thinking strictly from an adult perspective. They are excited that Kalid has so many options to learn. Kalid is discouraged that so many transitions are being asked of him. He is anxious, overwhelmed. Mom and Dad are afraid their son will not be successful without these new challenges.

- What can I do differently?

    Mom and Dad need to stop and listen to their son. Can they let go of their fear about his success? Can they make choices that help him feel protected? His eventual success in any area will come more easily if he feels protected and that his parents can place limits on themselves by taking his needs into account. As you can tell from the story, Mom and Dad were able to hold a position that both honored Kalid and honored their need to work and their desire that Kalid experience new things over the summer.

- If I have done the above, what do I need to learn more about that may be grounding my parental boat?

    Read more about temperament and the slow-to-warm-up child.

> **Theo's Unimportance**
>
> Theo is a second-born child with a much older sister. His parents, who had their children late in life, are dedicated to their children.
>
> Theo's older sister had some learning problems but with some help, graduated from high school and is in her third year at a university. However, Theo, in eighth grade, is getting D's in three subjects, even though his parents work regularly with him on his homework. They seem lost with Theo. They have missed the possibility of learning issues, seeing him instead as their argumentative child. They think of him as not wanting to perform as opposed to having blocks to his academic performance.

It is clear when I meet him that he is discouraged and does not believe in his own intelligence. He would like to quit school. Theo has numerous undiagnosed learning problems that neither he nor his parents understand and for which no one has sought help.

Theo, who is a skateboarder, beams when I talk to him about boarding. This is an area in which he feels competent. However, his father has already told me that he thinks boarders are losers who do drugs and listen to destructive hip-hop music. These associations are not based upon fact. He tells Theo he doesn't like him hanging out with his boarder friends.

Helping Theo not only involves helping him and his parents to understand his learning issues but to connect Theo and his parents around his boarding, where he feels good. His parents have to let go of their assumptions and see boarding through their son's eyes. Just because his friends wear baggy pants and listen to hip-hop does not necessarily mean they do drugs. I challenge Theo's parents to find some hip-hop with positive messages for their son. In appreciating his competence in boarding, they will strengthen their connection with him. This will help in handling much harder issues, such as his schoolwork.

- What is the problem?

Theo has an undiagnosed learning problem. His parents see him as argumentative and not wanting to perform at school.

- How old is the child?

He is thirteen years old and in eighth grade.

- What is happening with the child?

Theo currently has three D's in subjects at school. He has never been tested for learning problems. Theo is discouraged and does not think he is capable of passing his schoolwork.

HOW DO I USE THIS INFORMATION TO REACH MY GOAL?

- What channels need addressing?
  Theo is discouraged. He does not feel important.

- How do I, as a parent, contribute to this problem?
  Dad's relationship to Theo is discouraging of the one thing in which Theo feels competent: skateboarding. Dad is afraid skateboarding is only for "losers" and does not investigate his assumptions.
  After Dad has established a connection with Theo, he needs to show him he has his back. He needs to protect Theo from his own self-doubt. Finally, Dad needs to create a structure in which Theo can learn.

- What can I do differently?
  The first step is to get Theo tested so he can learn how he learns and can understand both his strengths and his weaknesses. Dad needs to discuss his fear of differentness. He needs to investigate skateboarding. Are his assumptions based upon fear?
  Finally, Mom and Dad can encourage Theo in areas in which he is competent. If there are areas in which he needs help, they can find a tutor for him. Set up a schedule of support.

- If I have done the above, what do I need to learn more about that may be grounding my parenting boat?
  Read Mel Levine's *A Mind at a Time*. Learn about learning styles and differences.

> **Molly's Story of Respect**
>
> Molly is very mature for her age. She has a younger brother and is a sophomore in high school on the A honor roll. She participates in the theater department, in debate, and on the student council.

> Molly's mother is a single parent who works hard at her professional career and prides herself on being there for her two children. Although Molly's dad lives in another state now, he lived near her for several years after the divorce and has lived with at least two women since the divorce. One of those women gave birth to a half-sister to Molly, but Dad never married the child's mother. It has become important to Molly's mother that she be present and available for her children, especially given what she perceives as Dad's inconsistent and sometimes immoral behavior.
>
> Molly comes into my office and is irate at Mom. Molly was asked by the French teacher to sign up for an elective at school as the teacher's assistant, a special honor seldom given to a sophomore. But Mom would not sign the permission slip. According to Molly, Mom didn't approve of her or her interests in language or the arts. Mom would only approve of her if she were to take more math or science. Molly said she did not believe she would ever be good enough for Mom unless she majored in math or science.

When I asked Mom to speak, she said she was worried the school might be misadvising Molly. She feared the teaching assistant job was only for the grading of papers and would be a waste of Molly's time. Mom further wondered what Molly would do to fulfill her math and science requirements. Mom was frightened she was not doing something or overlooking something else and that would lead to Molly's lack of success in college.

HOW DO I USE THIS INFORMATION TO REACH MY GOAL?

But when Mom began to talk about her pride in Molly and her excitement for her, the conversation changed. Respectfully, Mom asked Molly about her interests in languages, in the arts, and in being the teacher's assistant.

When Mom approached Molly with the respect that Molly had clearly earned by proving herself over time, Molly could begin to answer Mom's questions. It soon became clear that Mom had not understood the honor of being asked to assist the teacher. Instead, she had focused on her fears: her fear that the school might misadvise Molly, use her as free labor, distract her from academics, and perhaps prevent her admission into college.

When the conversation was based on love, Mom could ask her questions not out of fear but to seek more information. Then the conversation could add to their relationship, move away from a battle between trust and limits, and move toward feelings of importance and respect. Importance and respect need to be the cornerstone of parental conversations with an older adolescent.

- What is the problem?

    Mom is afraid that the teacher may be using Molly's skills and Molly will miss taking important courses if she helps the teacher. Molly is upset and thinks she will never be good enough for her mother.

- How old is the child?

    Molly is a sophomore in high school and is fifteen years old.

- What is happening in the child's world?

    Molly is a straight-A student. She takes some honors courses but not all. Molly has many extracurricular activities. All of them are in the language arts, theater arts, and leadership arenas. None of them are in the math and science areas.

- What channels need addressing?
    Respect and importance.
- How do I, as a parent, contribute to this problem?
    Mom is less trusting of other adults given Molly's father's past behavior. He has broken laws and does not act like a competent, caring adult. Therefore, Mom feels even more alone in her job as parent. Molly's mother feels isolated and solely responsible for Molly. She is afraid for Molly's future given her father's role-modeling. Molly's Mom is afraid Molly could be misadvised, which could limit her future options.

- What can I do differently?
    Mom needs to respect Molly's gifts and ways of belonging. Molly is a leader with linguistic and performance gifts. At this point, Molly does not choose to develop her math and science at an honors level. In demonstrating respect for Molly's passions, she also states that they are important. Mom grants true esteem for who Molly is as opposed to who she wants Molly to be.
    It is difficult as a parent to let go of our dreams of who our child should be and accept who they are. Once we do that, we can encourage them in their own talents to be all they can be.

- If I have done the above, what do I need to learn more about that may be grounding my parenting boat?
    Read more about adolescent brain development. Try David Walsh's *Why Do They Act That Way?* Read more about different forms of giftedness in Howard Gardner's *Frames of Mind*.

How does parenting style change over time?

Parenting is a job that by its very nature none of us will get completely right. We will all make mistakes. We will all question what is enough. We will all need to adjust the parenting boat many times and head back into the channels. Parenting is a balancing act not only between too much or too little but also between the parent and the child. That balancing act changes as the child grows. For the young child, the parent is an authority. We know more about the world and what is needed to navigate. It is okay to claim our authority. Claiming authority does not come from trying to control or exert power. It comes from inner strength. It is not a power struggle but calm assurance in leading a child into his future. Claiming that authority is best done from an authoritative stance as opposed to an authoritarian one. Certain children, due to temperament, etc., have a tendency toward power struggles with adults who are authoritarian in their approach.

As a child moves into adolescence, a conversation occurs, much like that of a coach with an athlete. We still know more and will exert consequences for behavior that affects the team. However, we try even harder to get the child to understand the reasoning, the values we are trying to teach. It is through understanding that we hope they will learn to act on those values when we are no longer present. It is through our coaching that we help them develop their own brain and the ability to preview consequences of their choices.

Finally, we take on the role of wise elders. The young adults' choices bear consequences for them to shoulder. Learning from their mistakes chisels them into the fine adults we value as members of our community. Those are the adults we may need to call upon to help with our decisions in our later years. If we do not let go, our children cannot grow into their full potential as adults. If we do not let go, they do not know or realize we believe in them. It is not abandonment, as helicopter parents often fear. Instead, it is a demonstration of faith in them at that point. That faith includes the knowledge that we have taught them to be courageous enough to ask for the help all adults need on occasion.

What does my child bring to the equation?
All children come into our lives with their own unique gifts and challenges. No one gets a pass. Even the very gifted, pleasing child must learn to strengthen a weak muscle of assertiveness. They need to learn there are times it is important to say, "No," even though another person may not be pleased. At the opposite end is the child whose weak muscle is a lack of empathy and cooperativeness due to negative moods or anxiety.

You, as a parent, are not responsible if your child is born with a learning disability, a challenging temperament, a mental illness, etc. Just as you are not responsible for your child's gifts in music, art, etc. However, you are responsible for helping your child learn to adjust to whatever gifts or challenges she possesses to grow into an adult who can function in our society. If your child has Down syndrome, that functioning will look different for him than for a child with autism or a child who needs to learn to use a very special gift. In some cases, your parenting boat will begin closer to the shoals. It is incumbent upon you to help steer that boat so you and your child can come as close as possible to the channels. In order to do that, you will need to overcome your own fears, your busyness, your lack of knowledge, etc.

No matter what gifts or challenges your child brings with him, it is still my hope to develop within him a sense of competence, caring, and contributing. This can be done to some extent no matter the challenge. Temple Grandin is an example of someone who had to overcome weaknesses to reach her goals.

To build *competence* in children is to create:
- a sense of self-discipline both in their behavior and in their emotions;
- a sense of their gifts and the steps necessary to further develop their gifts;

HOW DO I USE THIS INFORMATION TO REACH MY GOAL?

- a sense of their own ability to solve problems and a pride in their abilities to do so;
- a sense of courage to ask for help when needed;
- a belief that they can handle the world more and more as they grow;
- a refusal to allow a label—be it medical, educational, or psychological—to limit their belief in their own ability;
- an ever-increasing ability in us to let go of them;
- a sense of being their own people, not just being our children.

To build *caring* in children is to create:
- an ability to understand their impact upon others;
- a gratefulness for what they have and an appreciation that not all people have the same gifts, things, or resources;
- a recognition that all people are special;
- a recognition of differences between cultures, socioeconomic groups, ages, and countries and an ability to value those differences.

To engender *contributing* in children is to create:
- a sense that they are appreciated for what they do;
- a sense that they can do things well enough;
- an expectation that all members help in the family and in life according to their age and abilities;

- the belief, as stated by John D. Rockefeller, "I believe that every right implies a responsibility, every opportunity an obligation, every possession a duty."

Conclusion

The good news is that your parenting boat is usually a canoe, not the *Titanic*. When we find ourselves out of the channel we can always get back in the channel. Children are always learning. Hopefully adults are always learning. Keep faith. Watch the channel markers. Stay in the channels or work to get back in them.

Remember, as parents, lots of things affect the course of your boat: the wind, the channel depth, and the current. These are analogous to your child's strengths, weaknesses, temperament, biochemistry, brain, school, friends, fate, etc. This book is certainly not meant to blame parents. We don't need to take an already difficult job and make it harder through blame.

I am simply putting out markers to note when the canoe is out of the channel. All of the markers are based upon my view of what it takes to create a competent, caring, and contributing adult. My markers serve to clarify and aid in attaining that mission in parenting. It is my dream that we will all be able to walk through our fear and toward our mission. As always, I wish you well on your journey. We are all simply trying to be good enough as parents and as people.

References

Agel, Jerome. *The Radical Therapist*. New York: Ballantine Books, 1974.

Brazelton, T. Berry, and Joshua Sparrow. *Calming Your Fussy Baby: The Brazelton Way*. New York: Perseus, 2003.

Budd, Linda S. *Living with the Active Alert Child*, 3rd ed. Seattle, WA: Parenting Press, 2003.

Chess, Stella, and Alexander Thomas. *Know Your Child*. New York: Basic Books, 1987.

Clarke, Jean Illsley, Connie Dawson, and David Bredehoft. *How Much Is Enough? Everything You Need to Know to Steer Clear of Overindulgence and Raise Likeable, Responsible and Respectful Children*. New York: Marlowe & Co., 2004.

Erikson, Erik. *Childhood and Society*. New York: WW Norton, 1963.

———. *Insight and Responsibility*. New York: WW Norton, 1964.

Frankl, Viktor. *Man's Search for Meaning*. New York: Washington Square Press, 1963.

Gardner, Howard. *Frames of Mind: The Theory of Multiple Intelligences*. New York: Basic Books, 1993.

Gibran, Kahil. *The Prophet*. New York: Alfred A. Knopf, 1977.

Gilson, Dave. "We're All #1." *Mother Jones*. January/February, 2008.

Grandin, Temple. *The Way I See It: A Personal Look at Autism and Asperger's*. Arlington, TX: Future Horizons, 2008.

Grandin, Temple, and Sean Barron. *Unwritten Rules of Social Relationships*. Arlington, TX: Future Horizons, 2005.

Kranowitz, Carol S. *The Out-of-Sync Child: Recognizing and Coping with Sensory Processing Disorder.* Revised Ed. New York: Penguin Group, 2006.

Levine, Mel. *A Mind at a Time.* New York: Simon & Schuster, 2003.

Marano, Hara Estroff. "A Nation of Wimps." *Psychology Today.* November/December, 2004.

Munsch, Robert. *I Love You Forever.* New York: Firefly, 2001.

Schaub, Janette. *My Child Has ADHD: Now What? A Handbook for Parents, Educators and Practitioners.* Minneapolis, MN: Beaver's Pond Press, 1998.

Seuss, Dr. *Horton Hatches the Egg.* New York: Random House, 1968.

Sykes, Charles. *50 Rules Kids Won't Learn in School: Real-World Antidotes to Feel-Good Education.* New York: St. Martin's Press, 2007.

Walsh, David. *Why Do They Act That Way? A Survival Guide to the Adolescent Brain for You and Your Teen.* New York: Free Press, 2005.

Biography

Author of *Living With the Active Alert Child*, Dr. Linda S. Budd is an adjunct professor in Family Social Science at the University of Minnesota. A licensed psychologist, marriage and family therapist, and a registered play therapist, she has taught parenting for over thirty years, and is a well-known speaker. She has appeared many times on TV and radio, was a contributing writer for the Family Information Network for over a decade, and has been featured in many magazine and newspaper articles. Dr. Budd was presented with the Distinguished Teaching Award by the University of Minnesota and the Distinguished Service Award by the Minnesota Association of Marriage and Family Therapy. She was designated one of the Centennial One Hundred by the College of Human Ecology at the University of Minnesota, and was later honored with a Hall of Fame Award from Mt. Olive College, North Carolina. Dr. Budd lives in St. Paul, Minnesota, with her husband Jeffrey.

Made in the USA
Charleston, SC
16 November 2011